D1491196

MEDIA MARKETING

BOOKS BY PETER G. MILLER

THE COMMON-SENSE MORTGAGE

THE COMMON-SENSE GUIDE TO SUCCESSFUL
REAL ESTATE NEGOTIATION
(with Douglas M. Bregman)

MEDIA MARKETING

Peter G. Miller

MEDIA
MARKETING

*How to get your name
and story in print
and on the air*

1817

HARPER & ROW, PUBLISHERS   New York
Cambridge, Philadelphia, San Francisco, Washington
London, Mexico City, São Paulo
Singapore, Sydney

FIRST EDITION

Designer: Ruth Bornschlegel

Copy editor: Rick Hermann

Indexer: Maro Riofrancos

Library of Congress Cataloging-in-Publication Data
Miller, Peter G.
    Media marketing.
    Includes index.
    1. Mass media—Authorship. 2. Marketing. I. Title.
P96.A86M55 1987 659.2 87-45073
ISBN 0-06-055091-0   87 88 89 90 91 MPC 9 8 7 6 5 4 3 2 1
ISBN 0-06-096214-3 (pbk) 87 88 89 90 91 MPC 9 8 7 6 5 4 3 2 1

To Herman Albert Miller

Contents

PART FOUR   DEVELOPING MODEL PROGRAMS

Acknowledgments

Within the process of writing a book there are always critically important people who bring ideas and energy to a project. The first version of this material originally appeared in a series of 51 weekly columns published by the *Washington Business Journal* (Suite 930, 8200 Greensboro Drive, McLean, Virginia 22102). Former *Journal* editor Susan Courier reviewed and refined columns, debated issues and added much to the ultimate product.

I would not have met Susan, however, were I not introduced by Barbara Pomerance, Senior Vice-President of the Bethesda, Maryland, firm of Ehrlich-Manes & Associates, Inc. Barbara is a recognized professional, one of the very best people in media marketing, and her corporate and association clients are fortunate to have the benefit of her services.

Preface

Few industries are more visible yet less understood than the news media. We constantly see what someone, somewhere, has defined as "newsworthy," but how such decisions are made is largely a mystery. And since the process of turning data into news is so unclear, it's tough to get coverage because most of us don't know who to call or what to say.

As someone with experience as a writer and broadcaster, and as someone with experience as a promoter, I've seen both sides of the news gathering process. The system is rational, it does make sense and most people can earn coverage once they understand how it works.

This book is designed to serve as a promoter's introduction to the media. It assumes that you have given interests and that those interests can be enhanced or expanded through media coverage.

How news is defined, what reporters want and why promotion has become increasingly important are discussed in the first section. In the second, we look at how to find the right media, how to make contact with reporters and the subject of news releases, a wholly misunderstood form of communication.

In the third section we examine the interview process, news conferences and the specific needs of various media formats. The fourth section contains three model programs, one each for a retailer, a professional and an association. These brief models suggest strategies promoters can use in media marketing and the results such programs can produce.

PETER G. MILLER

Silver Spring, Maryland
March 1987

PART ONE

INSIDE MEDIA MARKETING

Few institutions are more ingrained in our daily lives than the media. We awake to the radio and read the morning paper. By day we scan magazines, newspapers and newsletters, and by night we tune in the evening news and read books. There's no doubt that much of our time is devoted to absorbing and reacting to what we read, see and hear.

But for many of us, it's not enough to just receive information. We want more from the media and by "more" we mean access. We want to appear in print and on the air. We want to promote our ideas, publicize our products and enhance our names. We want access for reasons of commerce and ego, because appearing in the media creates a certain cachet, importance, currency and credibility machines can't build and dollars can't buy.

Yet as much as we want media access, most efforts to reach print and broadcast outlets fail. An informal survey of one Washington news bureau showed that it received nearly 2,000 news releases, announcements and letters plus more than 100 telephone contacts—in a single week! Of all these pleas, pitches and petitions, not more than one or two percent ever found their way into print.

The story in newsrooms around the country is basically the same. Much time and substantial sums of money are spent developing campaigns that often produce few tangible results. Visit any news operation, whether it's print or broadcast, and you're certain to find piles of discarded news releases, unused photos and unread documents. Judging from the large number of promotional efforts that fail, it's clear few people understand how journalists work or why they choose one story and not another.

But while promotional failures are common, there are some corporations, some media marketing specialists, some organizations and some individuals who are successful, who receive positive coverage on a continuing basis.

How do they do it?

All promoters are different and the precise strategy that works for one may not work for another. Yet despite differences, successful promoters do have something in common: They behave within definable guidelines that can be observed, measured and copied by others.

This is a book about the media, how information is obtained, packaged and distributed and how you can obtain ongoing press coverage. Based on training, experience and observation over a period of more than twenty years, it argues that media access is not reserved for corporate giants or presidential candidates. You're important and reporters would like to hear from you, *but only if you know how the system works and how to package your ideas.* In turn, if more people are familiar with the news business, journalists will spend less time sorting through unusable news releases and unworkable story proposals.

1
WHY MEDIA MARKETING?

Understanding how the media works is not merely a matter of idle curiosity. Whether you're a manufacturer or a professional, part of a civic group or a governmental agency, a politician or retailer, having access to the media on a continuing, positive and productive basis is a decided advantage, one that can often be measured in terms of enhanced prestige, greater recognition and larger revenues.

Not only is an understanding of the media important today, but the probability is that such information will become increasingly important in the coming years. The reason: our growing development as an information-based society.

In his best-selling book *Megatrends,* John Naisbitt demonstrates how we have moved from an industrial society to an information society where the majority of our people—some 65 percent, according to Naisbitt—"create, process and distribute" information. In addition, Naisbitt makes this point:

> In an industrial society, the strategic resource is capital; a hundred years ago, a lot of people may have known how to build a steel plant, but not very many could get the money to build one. Consequently, access to the system was limited. But in our new society, as Daniel Bell first pointed out, the *strategic* resource is information. Not the only resource, but the most important. With information as the strategic resource, access to the economic system is much easier. (Emphasis his.)

5

If it's true that information is our new capital and we now have an information-based society, it's also true that information per se is not particularly valuable in isolation. A cure for cancer would be wonderful, but if the discovery is made by a hermit who refuses to share his secret, no one will benefit.

To have maximum value, information must be widely disbursed, freely received, evaluated in the context of other information and then redistributed after evaluation so the entire cycle can begin again. For this process to be successful, to avoid the problem of ideas in isolation, there must be lines of communication and those lines are what we call the "media."

The "media" can be defined as all devices and technologies allowing one person or entity to contact another. Specialized magazines, business weeklies, cable TV, books, company newsletters, morning newspapers, computer networks, neighborhood fliers, radio broadcasts and direct mail campaigns are all examples of the media.

MEDIA MARKETING DEFINED

With so many media outlets available, and with so much demand by those outlets for stories and ideas, there must be a reasonable process to obtain coverage on a consistent basis. There is such a process—a body of principles, concepts and approaches we'll call "media marketing." Media marketing can be defined as strategies and actions designed to enhance products, persons, events, ideas and organizations through positive media attention year after year.

The expression "media marketing" is probably less familiar than the term "public relations." But "media marketing" seems more appropriate for several reasons.

Within the field of public relations are many people capable of developing successful promotional campaigns and packaging ideas that attract media attention. Indeed, within the public relations field are individuals with extensive media backgrounds who could vie just as easily for jobs in journalism if they so elected.

Yet the term "public relations" carries excess baggage which makes it less appealing or precise than "media marketing." Yes, there are knowledgeable professionals in public relations, but public relations is not a defined field, such as law or medicine, and the expression "public relations" is often used in an unflattering context.

To practice law or medicine, or to be a plumber, accountant, barber, embalmer or whatever, you need a license. And by having a licensure requirement there is a presumption of training, experience and a basic standard of performance.

In public relations (and in journalism) there are no licensure laws, a situation which has its positive points. Unnecessary degrees, irrelevant tests and the general problem of excess "credentialism" are avoided. Anyone can enter the field, including people who champion unpopular causes and unorthodox ideas.

Having no licensure rules also means something else: Anyone can claim to be "in public relations" and as a consequence the term is used widely. Not only might someone "in public relations" be a communication or marketing expert; the description may also refer—judging from various classified advertisements—to telephone solicitors, receptionists and individuals with attractive personalities and a driver's license.

The public relations professionals in whom we are most interested obviously do not act as telephone solicitors or receptionists. They have a sizable array of skills and expertise and to describe more precisely their interests and activities it makes sense to use a more specific term than "public relations." "Media marketing" comes closest to describing the areas that interest us most: understanding how journalists work and how ideas can be packaged for maximum exposure.

There is another reason the term "public relations" seems inappropriate. It's ironic that the very phrase "public relations" often has a negative connotation. We hear and read about "PR stunts" or that the position of a political candidate is "just public relations." Egomaniacs are said to "believe their own PR."

These expressions devalue an important concept. *People and organizations have an innate right to present themselves as best they can and to appear in the media as frequently as they can generate interest.* There's nothing wrong, unfair or unethical with such self-interest. If self-interest is so terrible, why then do so many newspapers, magazines and broadcast outlets have active public relations departments? Such organizations obviously recognize that media marketing is a valuable tool in the ongoing race for more distinction, greater circulation and higher ratings.

But rather than grouping ideas under a value-laden term that's not always admired, it may be best to start with a fresh expression, one without negative connotations. "Media marketing" is both descriptive and precise; it goes no further than it should and excludes a variety of unrelated activities and interests.

THE IMPORTANCE OF MEDIA ACCESS

If we are now in an information-based society, if Naisbitt, Bell and others are right, then access to the media—the crucial web by which we all communicate—is critically important. Here's why.

First, the success of many ideas, organizations, events or products can only be maximized with media attention. Personal success, in a material sense, may also be tied to media access.

Consider the case of a suburban area where two new hardware stores open at the same time. At Dunn's, there's a grand-opening sale, big banners and 20-percent discounts.

At the other store, Lyle & Stokes, the owners also have arranged for a grand opening. They, too, offer discounts and have big banners. But beyond the usual hoopla, they're having a home crafts fair with such events as wallpaper contests (who can paper a 4 × 8 panel fastest), nail-driving events for teenagers (who can hammer a single nail in the fewest blows, who can hammer the most nails in 60 seconds), a display of woodwork from local craftsmen and a used tool auction where all proceeds go to the community hospital. In addition, they've contacted masons, carpenters, plumbers, electricians and professionals from 20 other trades and listed them in a directory which will be given to consumers at no cost.

If you're a reporter for the local paper, which store makes a better feature? If you're an assignment editor at a local TV station, which store offers the better visuals? If you're a consumer, which store will you hear about and which are you more likely to patronize? And finally, if you're a local mason, plumber or carpenter, which store would you prefer, the one that sells the same items as every other hardware store or the firm that puts your name before the public?

Second, those with continuing media access will have more opportunities for success than those without access or those lacking frequent coverage.

Too often the effort to gain media attention is limited to a one-time promotion and then dropped. Media marketing is and should be an ongoing process. Toys, for instance, receive much attention around Christmas and yet toys are sold year-round. Recognizing that the public follows movie and video sales on a regular basis, suppose Burnham's Toys compiles a monthly best-seller list divided by age group to help adults select children's gifts.

Ask yourself, if you're a local editor, would you want a monthly listing of top-selling toys? It's a novel feature, one potentially valuable to a broad readership segment. If a friend's son is having a birthday in June, would there not be value to a list of best-selling toys? And, if Burnham's provides the latest statistics and comments on the newest trends, why shouldn't they be cited as a source?

Third, promotional skills are essential in many fields where products and services are largely indistinguishable.

In the eternal search for market distinction, individuals and businesses try to stand out in the midst of "competitive clutter." Because a large number of substantially similar choices are available in most fields, it's difficult for consumers, users, buyers or clients to objectively select one competitor and not another. Since the alternatives are basically alike, there are no "wrong" choices and therefore *decisions are often made on the basis of familiarity and name recognition, major by-products of media attention.*

If we're buying steel ingots there is little competitive clutter. Ingots can be tested, priced, compared and physically held. In many fields, however, distinctions are less clear. One result is that we're encouraged to have brand loyalty, not because we particularly benefit, but because brand names are often the only way the products of one manufacturer can be distinguished from those of another.

Blindfold 100 people, have them ride in cars of similar size and cost, and the probability of their matching an auto's comforts and ride with specific brand names is just about zero. The story is much the same with adhesive bandages, writing paper, photocopies, clothes washers, paper tissues, gasoline, eyeglass lenses, canned corn and tires, to cite a few examples. Indeed, it's entirely common for one factory to produce identical products which are then marketed under different, and sometimes competing, labels.

The world of services is even more perplexing. Professions have a way of homogenizing their practitioners. The person who finishes at the top of his or her class in medical school and the individual with the lowest passing grades are both known by the same title after graduation: Doctor. For the public, it's tough to tell who's best, who's the most competent or why one should be selected over another.

Unlike choosing a shipment of ingots, the issue historically has not been pricing (many service providers have had a curious pattern of identical charges) or quality (licensure means that every provider meets a set of qualifications high enough to bar broad competition but not so tough that every provider rivals Einstein). Instead, the selection of one service provider over another is commonly linked to word-of-mouth recommendations from others, and to convenience.

If there are 100 lawyers in town and you need a will, which attorney do you choose? They all went to law school.

They all graduated and passed a standardized bar exam. So who do you select? The one nearby? The one with the fanciest furniture—and perhaps the highest fee? The one your neighbor used?

As hard as it may be for service users to make distinctions among service providers, it's also difficult for providers themselves to demonstrate differences. In the modern sense, there is little marketing experience in many fields, in part because until recently licensure laws often banned advertising as "undignified" or "unprofessional," terms which really mean, "Hey, we've got a good thing here, don't upset the apple cart." Not incidentally, marketing prohibitions helped maintain monopolistic prices, reduced advertising costs, limited the ability of newcomers to compete and protected minimally adept practitioners, the 50 percent in every profession who are less than average.

Now, however, marketing is widespread in every field and profession, prices in many specialties have declined, but to a surprising degree at least one old problem remains: How do you find the best lawyer, doctor, dentist or optometrist?

What has really happened is that we've replaced one form of clutter with another. Before, it was hard to choose professionals because there were few objective standards by which they could be judged. Now it's hard to judge professionals because advertising tells us not who is best, but who is available.

Given few objective clues, a consumer may well opt to buy from the car manufacturer who wins the most races and gets the most name recognition, rather than the firm which quietly concentrates on building a better vehicle. The physician quoted in the sports pages will receive more referrals for sore necks than the unknown doctor who makes little effort to market his services. The attorney who writes a weekly legal-affairs column will stand out, not necessarily because he is—or is not—the world's leading legal authority in a given specialty, but because his name is familiar.

Fourth, we increasingly define importance by the extent

of media coverage received. If it's not in the media it isn't important. Conversely, receiving media coverage creates importance.

Suppose we have two candidates for political office. Barringer is athletic, telegenic, speaks well and has faithfully memorized 26 position papers prepared by his advisers. Springer, his primary opponent, is 90 pounds overweight, wears suits long out of style and has an entire campaign based on two fliers typed at home.

Who gets the most attention? Barringer. Why? Because he's a media-oriented candidate. His ideas on a variety of subjects, or at least his advisers' ideas, have been carefully prepared and written out. Every night another 20-second bite from his stump speech is used on TV. Barringer is seen as the "stronger" candidate because he gets more exposure, and, in circular fashion, because he gets more exposure he *is* the stronger candidate. If Springer ever won, his victory would be described as a "major upset," not because he beat a necessarily better candidate but because he defeated someone with greater media access.

Fifth, whether a story is covered, how it's reported and how long coverage continues each influences public perception.

When the Ohio savings and loan system was stuck with a well-publicized loss in the mid-1980s, hordes of depositors rushed to withdraw funds from S&Ls throughout the state. The rush for funds, inspired though it was by the perception of a massive drain on the state insurance program, created an actual crisis within the Ohio S&L system. The governor was forced to first close more than seventy institutions for a "banking" holiday and to then reopen them only when the withdrawal rights of depositors were limited. A somewhat similar situation developed in Maryland, this time because fraud at a major S&L precipitated a run on that state's S&Ls. Here again, the perception of loss hurt other S&Ls throughout the state, even though most were well run and entirely secure.

Sixth, media coverage allows perceptions to be com-

*municated more rapidly and more widely than might other-
wise be possible.*

If the problems in Ohio and Maryland were known only
to a few regulatory experts, they might have talked among
themselves, but there would not have been an immediate,
widespread run on entire S&L systems. Media coverage did
not create the lender's initial problems, but it assuredly con-
tributed to the increased withdrawals from honest, well-run
S&Ls.

Seventh, media coverage creates perceptions.

In the mid-1980s the media quoted various sources who
suggested that as many as 1.5 million children were "missing" each year, reports which created enormous public concern. But the figures were grotesque, wholly unsubstantiated
estimates. FBI records at the time showed fewer than 100
kidnappings nationwide in the course of an entire year.

By not giving the full story, by not putting numbers in
perspective, many people were unduly worried and concerned. The perception of a massive problem became widespread, while the reality—although hardly comforting—was
ignored.

*Eighth, to gain media attention, size and money are im-
portant, but not as important as creativity and packaging.*

Media marketing is among the most democratic activities we have. Anyone can play; you don't need a huge inheri-
tance or a powerful job to gain press attention, though certainly such assets are helpful.

What journalists want are story concepts to interest their
readers, viewers and listeners. If you've got such an idea, if
you know how to package it, the probability of getting coverage is excellent. If you haven't got a workable idea, then
money, power and position are worth little. Wastepaper bas-
kets in newsrooms around the country are filled with releases
from the nation's largest firms and most prestigious institutions, organizations which—despite their size and dollars—
failed to understand the media's essential needs.

An actual example: While most taxi fares are calculated
by meters, cabs in Washington, D.C., charge on a zone sys-

tem. The more zones you cross, the higher the fare. The system is so confusing that few people understand how it works, particularly tourists and foreign visitors. But when cabbie Novell B. Sullivan self-published an 86-page guide to the city's zone system, The Washington *Post* ran a large story complete with Sullivan's picture and a zone map. Sullivan succeeded not because he had a $1 million promotional budget or a staff of highly paid experts, but because he had a sound idea that would interest *Post* readers.

Some may read these words and argue that while promotion is important, you don't need journalists to appear in print or on the air. Why bother with media marketing when you can buy as much space and time as you want, or at least as much as you can afford? The answer, as we shall explain in the next chapter, is that advertising and editorial coverage involve markedly different values.

2

ADS VERSUS MEDIA MARKETING

Media access is most often seen in terms of advertising. If you want to reach a particular audience, the easiest and most direct approach is to buy space or time in the media of your choice.

Advertising is a multibillion-dollar industry and it's hard to believe a business of such size is possible without an observable record of success. Certainly advertising does offer benefits; each year selected products and services increase sales and expand their market share because of successful ad campaigns.

Yet the concept of advertising is not always attractive or plausible. It presumes, by definition, that would-be advertisers have money to spend, an unlikely situation for new firms, companies operating at a loss or organizations with limited revenues.

Even if you have the money to advertise, there are still problems. Audiences must be defined, themes and concepts developed and the entire presentation packaged in a creative manner. Given these requirements, developing productive ads isn't simple nor are results guaranteed.

Ads must also be placed with great care. Not only do ads compete among themselves for the time and attention of readers, viewers and listeners, they also compete with the editorial material they surround.

If you're an advertiser, you want your ad to appear in a successful medium that attracts a specific audience. Yet, ironically, you don't want a medium that's "too" successful. Such a publication or program will attract many ads, and yours may not stand out in such a saturated environment. At the same time, you also don't want a medium offering such riveting editorial content that your ad is ignored, a concern which may explain, for example, the mundane nature of so much television programming.

For many people, money alone is the difference between advertising and media marketing. The only problem with this quick and neat distinction is accuracy: "Free" promotion, in an absolute sense, is an illusion.

Although media coverage may be free, the expense of obtaining such exposure is not. Whether you do it yourself or hire professionals, it takes time, preparation and considerable thinking to generate worthwhile media exposure.

If media marketing is not free, then how much is it worth? Why can't you place a price tag on media marketing efforts by calculating the cost for equivalent advertising space? Suppose you can buy advertising space at $100 per column inch in a metropolitan daily. Shouldn't a 15-inch story be valued at $1,500?

In statistical terms it's certainly possible to calculate the value of media marketing coverage if our standard is raw space and air time. The problem, however, is that we're attempting to compare radically different concepts.

Advertising is unfiltered communication that allows you to control the content of your message. Short of libel, crazed medical claims or bigotry, you can say whatever you want and most media outlets will run your ad untouched. With media marketing, you rely on journalists to interpret your story.

Advertising allows you to place an ad any day or, if you like, every day. For a premium, you can often assure which page or section will carry your ad. With media marketing not only is timing unsure, but it's impossible to project when an article will appear—if at all—or whether a broadcast will air. Worse still, even if you obtain coverage, you can't be sure what will be presented; you have no control over the length, content, style, placement or context of whatever is being printed or broadcast.

When comparing advertising to media marketing the distinctions above seem to give a significant edge to advertising. But there is another value to consider: the nature of communication.

Advertising is an adversarial form of contact. Somebody is trying to sell something and no matter how well presented, advertising is advertising. Even so-called "institutional" advertisements—the messages that tell us to drive safe, drink less or give more to charity—are adversarial in the sense that advertisers seek to enhance their names by associating with a particular public concern. If institutional efforts are meant as purely munificent gestures, then surely there is no reason why the financing of such ads can't be anonymous.

Media marketing is not an adversarial form of communication precisely because it's filtered through independent journalists and their editors or news directors. The public reads, watches and listens with the expectation that working journalists have gathered the news for us. If they write or broadcast information about a particular subject, we assume there must be some news value in the topic. News articles and broadcasts are not perceived as places where goods and services are sold or as forums where coverage can be bought, and therefore information which appears in the news is not regarded as adversarial communication.

Suppose a software firm spends $10,000 advertising its product in computer publications and receives 150 responses. Suppose also that a review of the company's software by a leading computer magazine generates 800 queries.

Is it possible the firm's ads are merely ineffective? Sure. Another reason, however, is that people resist salesmanship. The very act of selling, in and of itself, causes us to raise our defenses. But since news articles and broadcasts are not commonly perceived as marketing tools, the public has no reason to be defensive and therefore a major barrier to acceptance is removed.

Advertising tells the world how you want to be regarded, but when you're the subject of press attention, it's the media making an evaluation. With positive editorial coverage from an independent media outlet, you gain the implicit, undeniable sanction and approval of the publication or program that carries your story, an entitlement that cannot be fully valued in the same way that we price column inches or minutes of air time. And, it should be said, it's an entitlement that can't be bought.

3
WHAT IS NEWS?

Trying to define the term "news" is somewhat like watching a magician pulling scarves from a thimble. First there's a small wisp of color and soon yards and yards of material follow. The concept of "news" is equally baffling: What seems clear and obvious up-front turns out to be surprisingly complex.

Knowing how to define "news" is not merely an academic exercise; it's essential for those wanting press coverage. The media has an innate interest in news and it follows that if what you're doing or saying is "news," the media will also have an interest in you. But what is news?

Perhaps the best way to test the news value of a particular story is to paraphrase an ancient question: What makes a person, event, product, idea or organization different from all others? Information without distinction is data, not news.

"News," in the most basic sense, is simply information you didn't have before. When you first hear the local football team is ahead 21–6 in the third quarter or that your favorite hardware store was robbed, that's news.

But if it's true that "news" is fresh information, it's also true that some news is both known and aged. On New Year's Day, you can find any number of "year in review" reports telling you things you already know. Weekly and monthly magazines routinely recount "old" news, albeit with information and perspectives that may not have been available at the time of the event. Reporters rewrite old information and create background pieces so breaking news (new news?) can be seen in perspective. A given event can produce ten different stories, each with a different perspective oriented toward a specific audience. Commentators take old information, add their opinions, and create columns and editorials. These commentaries, in turn, may themselves evolve into news by raising new ideas and perspectives.

Whether old or new, news is also information tailored to a specific audience, or "public." Suppose a plane crashes at a major metropolitan airport. That information may make the local paper's front page. The same accident could also create a business article detailing the finances of the plane's corporate owners; a regulatory article discussing how governmental agencies are responding—or have responded in the past—to the type of problem that caused the crash; an airline safety feature in a major national magazine; a review of airplane claims processing in an insurance magazine; a first-person account in a popular monthly magazine; a feature on airport disaster services in a medical journal and ongoing daily and weekly broadcast accounts as the accident is investigated over time.

So now we can define news as new information, old information, repackaged information, expanded or condensed information, information that's the subject of commentary, personalized information, time-sensitive information, information placed in context, entertaining information, information oriented toward a specific audience and information that for one reason or another is considered unique to a particular audience. In essence, the concept of news is so wondrously elastic that almost any information is news somewhere. But if virtually every smidgen of information can be defined as news, why are so few promotional efforts successful?

Although information per se can be news, for a story to be usable it must also offer *utility, placement* and *proper packaging.*

Utility means being at the right media at the right time. A new product that blocks excessive suntanning is likely to draw little attention with a February news release in Buffalo. It's potentially news but it's not particularly useful. The same

BETTERING THE ODDS:
Seven Basic Approaches to Story Building

It's always news when the circus comes to town or a new teenage spelling champ is proclaimed, even though everyone has heard these stories before. Such events are newsworthy only because promoters have taken standardized stories and added a little spice, a new twist and some updating to make them current. Here are seven quick ways to embellish potential stories.

Does it conflict? Disagreements, court battles, disputes, discord, splits and divisions all make good stories.

Is it extreme? The mundane and the usual become newsworthy when the right adjectives are added. We're interested in things and events that are larger, smaller, longer, wider, heavier, lighter, first, last, faster, slower, younger and older. The shortest guy in the NBA and the biggest convention in town both get coverage.

Is it dated? Is it happening now, later, tomorrow or never? Currency makes news, and events related to a given date can also be newsworthy. A newly discovered set of Lincoln's papers will make headlines. Bigger headlines are possible if the discovery is announced on the Great Emancipator's birthday.

Is it a milestone? We relate to markers such as the town's 100th anniversary, the one millionth album and the score of the last game. Give a story a milestone and you've created a news peg.

Is it localized? Floods in our hometown are news, floods in Peru are less interesting. The floods, and the potential for tragedy, are identical, but location influences our interest level.

Is it specialized? Does it affect my profession, religion, club or industry? We are each unique, but we are each part of many publics. The Methodist carpenter who collects stamps and vacations in Bermuda is part of

continued

at least four identifiable groupings. He's a Methodist, a carpenter, a stamp collector and a Caribbean vacationer. An event that touches one of these four special interests may be newsworthy to him, but perhaps less so to the Catholic attorney who bowls weekly and vacations in Canada. The attorney has his own set of special interests.

Does it help? Devise a story that tells people "how to" and you'll get coverage. Favorites include how to save money, make money, lose weight, find romance, stay healthy, be popular, keep fit and stay young.

story in Tampa might make a general, medical or business feature at any time of year.

Even if a news release has news value, that value shrinks to zero if the release is sent to the wrong publication or station. Placement counts, and it pays to carefully examine each media contact before sending out releases. If a local college just raised $15 million to build a new gym, that may be news for local media or an alumni publication. But for a forestry magazine, chemical industry newsletter or city magazine 200 miles away, the story is likely to land in the dumper.

Most importantly, news values can be defined long before a news release is ever mailed. In creating media materials, individuals and organizations can strongly influence their promotional potential by the way they package stories.

Consider this example. A small manufacturer, Mr. Fulton, has developed a new oven that cuts heating costs and speeds cooking. He could send out a news release announcing his new product and then rely on various reporters to find a suitable angle to make the story newsworthy. Journalists, however, can choose from lots of good stories. Fulton will have a far better chance for coverage if he sees that his oven is more than just a new product. It implies a number of news possibilities that can be developed by writing several sets of

AUTHORITY FIGURES

While packaging is part of the promotion game, another part depends on the status of the packager. "Authority figures," people who can be identified in some way, are important in journalism because covering, quoting or citing them gives depth and credibility to stories. In a society obsessed with credentials, the "man on the street" and the "housewife from Peoria" represent the common man, and are seldom accorded coverage. The company president, the elected official, the college professor, the society-ball chairperson, the town doctor, the union leader, the minister, the rabbi, the judge and the Indian chief all receive regular coverage because of the positions and constituencies they represent.

What if you're not a doctor, Indian chief or elected official? Can you still be an authority figure?

The role of authority figure is an equal-opportunity position; everyone qualifies or can qualify, if they choose.

To be an authority figure there must be some reason that you're quotable. If it happens that you don't have a law degree or high position in industry, don't worry. It's okay to create your own credentials.

For instance, contribute to an industry journal or self-publish your own booklets and pamphlets. You'll have a quotable something to send reporters.

Give a speech. Speeches convey an element of authority and importance. Speaking engagements are available everywhere, all the time. Try clubs, associations, professional societies and industry groups for speaking dates. You'll need a cover letter and program outline to get booked.

Letters to the editor are popular, widely read and sure to attract media attention. Be brief, concentrate on one subject, quote sources to back-up your viewpoint, and criticize, if appropriate, in a respectful manner.

continued

> Teach. Give courses and seminars through community groups, professional organizations, adult-education services, junior colleges and noncredit schools. There's a constant search for good instructors, people with real-world experience and solid teaching skills.
>
> Lastly, get stationery, call a few friends and create your own organization. If you're bothered by phone rates, it's easier to get coverage if you're president of the "Southlawn Citizens Association" than if you're a lone telephone user.

promotional materials. If Fulton is shrewd he will make his story more competitive by offering a fresh angle to each reporter.

Different angles, or news "pegs," can be used to promote Fulton's oven to separate publics; that is, locally ("Fulton Develops New Oven, Area Employment to Rise"), regionally ("High-Tech Invades County"), as a consumer story ("More Heat, Lower Bills Power New Oven"), for a local business newspaper ("Fulton Outlook Heats Up with New Oven"), as a cooking feature ("Fulton Offers 20 New Recipes for High-Tech Oven"), for a national appliance-industry publication ("Buyers Back in Stores to See Fulton Oven") or as a feature for homemakers ("Fulton Oven Saves Time, Dollars"). For the broadcast media, one could easily see the oven demonstrated on daytime TV shows or discussed on radio call-in programs.

By segmenting his market and packaging his appeals, Fulton's story can attract greater media coverage than would be possible with a single, all-purpose news release. For Fulton, or for you, properly defining and packaging stories before they reach reporters is a decided advantage in the fight for media time and attention.

4
WHO SHOULD DEFINE THE NEWS

In the mid-1980s a new type of media blitz began, a campaign where the prize was not merely coverage but outright control of a national television network. Senator Jesse Helms (R-NC) and a group named Fairness in Media asked "almost one million" conservatives to invest their dollars in CBS stock and elect corporate directors who would "put an end to liberal media bias."

Whether one agrees with Helms or not, his proposal raises complex issues: Does the pattern of media ownership limit or enhance the free flow of ideas and information? Who should ultimately decide what's news and what isn't?

CBS is a media conglomerate that had sales of $4.92 billion in 1984. Its holdings at that time included five television stations, 11 radio stations and a network linking approximately 200 of the nation's 1,200 TV outlets. It owned general circulation magazines, cable TV interests and produced records under such labels as "Columbia" and "Epic."

In this mass of companies, subsidiaries and services, CBS News was the focus of attention. Was, or is, CBS News liberal? If so, what is "liberal"? If by some standard we can describe "liberal," and if CBS News is "liberal," how exactly are news judgments affected? Would news stories be more "biased" or less "biased" if CBS News were "conservative," assuming someone could explain what "conservative" means? What would it take for TV news to be "objective" and who is to define that term? How, in practice, does "objective" differ from "liberal" or "conservative"?

Suppose that Helms, himself a former TV broadcaster, gained control of CBS. How would CBS have changed? Would company shareholders have benefited if the firm's rock 'n' roll empire was sold off? What about news coverage? Is there a single, monolithic "objective" viewpoint represented by Senator Helms, or is there a diversity of positions regarding any given issue?

Throughout American history there have been avowed political publications and in a sense the Helms effort to take over CBS follows in this tradition. As examples, William Lloyd Garrison (1805–1879) published the *Liberator,* a paper opposed to slavery. William Randolph Hearst (1863–1951) used his papers to encourage the Spanish-American War. Today publications favoring a variety of political, social, economic and religious viewpoints are available in every community.

Basically Helms asked how TV news stories—and by inference radio and print stories as well—should be selected and presented, matters of importance to every promoter. His approach would rely on corporate management to establish policies, practices and guidelines for news departments.

Imagine, though, if news departments were not independent. Would efforts to ban alcohol commercials from television be reported fully? Or at all? Would attempts to limit TV violence or children's advertising be properly covered? Would commercial programming be publicized by network newscasters?

At some point in every field there must be a person who makes decisions, who has responsibility. We have judges who review laws and doctors who recommend treatments, and we also have journalists who define what's news and what isn't news for a particular publication or program.

No one argues that the decisions made by journalists are perfect or can be perfect, however one defines "perfection." News reporting is a subjective field where many views are possible, and that, in large measure, is why we have so many media outlets. But journalism should be left to journalists, however imperfect, rather than business tycoons, political theorists or other vested interests. One may not always agree with the judgments made by independent reporters, but at least such decisions are not made with other obligations in mind.

5
WHAT TO EXPECT
FROM REPORTERS

While the advantages of media attention are attractive—at least on occasion—the idea of contacting reporters may seem foreign. In a society where "tooting one's horn" is seen in a negative context, the idea of calling or writing a total stranger to promote oneself or one's story may seem pushy, egocentric and tasteless.

There is also the problem of who you're contacting. Don't reporters spend their time muckraking? Aren't they the folks who unearth scandals, find government waste and televise shoddy business practices? If you phone or write a reporter, won't you get nosy questions in return?

As with any profession, reporters have certain obligations to those they serve, but with journalism such obligations are often obscured by public perceptions. We tend to see the glamour of journalism rather than the grinding realities. At best, much of journalism can be described as labor intensive—there is nothing exciting about attending lengthy hearings, reading voluminous files or making dozens of phone calls while researching stories.

Then, of course, few professions are subject to such intense public scrutiny. Critics are everywhere and not all are particularly lucid. At least one radio talk-show host has been gunned down in the last few years.

What can you expect when dealing with reporters? Will reporters listen to your ideas or will you be ignored? Here are several observations.

• Don't expect to speak with a secretary. Print reporters typically answer their own phones, do their own typing and open their own mail. You can speak with just about any writer directly, but neither a postage stamp nor the cost of a phone call earns you an unlimited commitment of journalistic time or attention. Access to television reporters, particularly anchor personnel, tends to be more restricted.

• Don't worry about enlightened self-promotion. If you've got an idea that can be a good story and it happens coincidentally that you benefit, that's not a problem. If your idea is entirely self-serving, don't plan a long conversation.

• Don't expect to see a story before it's in print or on the air. If a subject is technical and complex the reporter will either be competent enough to handle the topic or will ask for clarification. Remember that journalists often cover regular beats or work for specialized publications. They have ongoing access to experts in every field, and by virtue of their training and experience many are regarded as authorities in their own right.

• Recognize that the publication or broadcast of "feature" material—stories not time-sensitive like breaking news—will often be delayed.

• Don't expect writers to send copies of their work. The presumption is that you normally see the publication anyway. One exception: Reporters for distant publications not available locally will often mail clips as a matter of courtesy.

• With large publications do not expect a reporter on one beat to write about a topic usually covered by someone else. Turf and territory are important. The same proposition holds true at radio and TV stations.

• Competition in journalism is ongoing and universal, a process sometimes called "creative tension." Journalistic competition includes not only external battles—one magazine versus another or one radio station against a second station—but also internal fights between individuals, staffs and sections. Success is measured by prestige assignments, column inches, air time and placement. If you've got a story that will lead page one, the reporter who writes it will look good to colleagues and peers—at least today. Conversely, the reporter who does great work for a year and is then less productive can be fired. There may be tenure in teaching and job security in many fields, but journalism isn't one of them.

• Recognize that the editorial process is complex and the interest of a single reporter may not assure coverage. A local television station, for instance, may have assignment editors, reporters, anchors and producers involved in the decision to use a particular item. Their preferences may be delayed or overturned if a hot story breaks, an executive producer dislikes the topic or a camera crew isn't available.

• Don't be surprised if you hear from a variety of people as a result of media coverage. Reporters constantly check competing media, a process called "research," so you're likely to receive calls from other journalists as a result of one article or broadcast.

• Be aware that even though you may have spent time with a reporter, been interviewed and supplied information, it doesn't obligate a reporter to use your material, accept your views or do a story. In essence, you're a seller in a buyer's market.

6
HOW BIG PLAYERS GET COVERAGE

There aren't many days when the news does not cover massive organizations. When a large corporation opens a new factory, the Red Cross seeks blood, a union strikes or the local government raises taxes, many people are affected and by definition such events are news.

That giant organizations are well covered by the media is hardly surprising. Much of our news concerns events and activities only large enterprises can organize or develop. Stories about a $700-million chemical plant are likely to feature gargantuan corporations rather than minor subcontractors.

Size alone does not make our giant organizations newsworthy, however. In the competition for media time and attention, large organizations often enjoy continuing media access because they can be readily covered by the media. And immediate access, in turn, is a fundamental consideration in the process of choosing stories.

Suppose a plane crashes in Washington, D.C. killing 30 people. On the same day, a mine disaster in a remote Montana valley results in an equal number of deaths. Both are terrible tragedies, but you can be certain the plane crash will draw far more attention.

Why? Because the Washington crash offers immediate access. The nation's capital is a major media center and so reporters and camera crews already in town can be routed to the crash site. Film can be developed and edited immediately while reporters on the scene provide live updates as new information is received.

As for the mine disaster, it surely deserves coverage, but

it takes so long to send cameras and reporters to the scene that the element of immediacy is lost. Even though "long" may be just a few hours in this example, in the competition for media time and space the mine disaster loses. Figure the Montana accident for extensive local coverage, but elsewhere it will rate a short story on day one, a follow-up with photo on day two and possibly a few paragraphs in a national news magazine a week later, perhaps as the lead for a general article on mine safety.

In less dramatic fashion, large organizations also offer immediate access. They arrange their affairs so reporters can easily obtain information, interviews, files and photos on short notice. Knowledgeable media specialists—often former journalists—keep reporters abreast of new developments, respond to media inquiries and suggest story ideas. Some organizations even advertise their availability as sources and list company contacts in media journals.

To see how immediate access works on a practical basis, consider the case of a real estate reporter writing about local housing trends. There are hundreds of area realty companies, and potentially a reporter could look in the phone book, pick names at random and see what different brokers might say. And although such random calls can occur, the reporter also knows that three major firms with active media information operations dominate the local market, each maintains extensive sales reports and each has a knowledgeable, quotable spokesman who can discuss current sales trends.

How did the reporter know about the company studies or who to contact?

• One presumes large firms in certain fields have specialized information relating to their own activities.

• Large firms routinely have information specialists who contact journalists and make sure reporters know what the company is doing. The very effort to reach the media, in and of itself, influences news coverage.

• It's easier and quicker to call three familiar sources who know how to work with the media than to unearth new contacts at random, particularly when deadlines loom.

• *Not* contacting large firms in a given field could result in a weak or incomplete story.

• Journalists who regularly cover individual "beats" such as housing develop sources over time and know who is a good contact and who isn't. The companies above have probably been sources in the past.

• Reporters may have heard or seen information elsewhere and are now following up with their own stories.

Although the "immediate" access created by large organizations seems to benefit both reporter and subject, the process contains two sizable flaws.

First, many large organizations have articulate, professional information specialists who constantly update reporters. Indeed, information from such sources is so voluminous that some journalists can probably sit back and cover certain industries just on the basis of handouts they receive.

But continually getting information from a limited number of sources creates a problem: If reporters use too much material from one source—even if that information is the best available—readers, listeners and viewers may wonder where the reportorial effort begins and the company information program ends, or how one can tell the difference between the two.

Second, although "immediate" access is convenient, often helpful and certainly the right approach for firms and organizations, "immediate" should not be confused with "complete" or "unbiased" access. For general stories to be accurate, fair and in context, it takes more information—and viewpoints—than a single source can readily provide. Conversely, if immediate access does nothing more than allow large organizations, or anyone, to gain a hearing for their views, that's a substantial advantage in the battle for media time and attention.

7

IS THERE ROOM FOR
THE LITTLE GUY?

With all the resources commanded by large companies, associations and governmental agencies, it would seem as though individuals and small organizations could not compete for media attention. After all, don't big organizations dominate the media, if only because they're so large?

In a word, no.

Every year *Fortune* magazine identifies the 500 largest American companies, the very organizations that should dominate the media, if domination were possible, on the basis of size, resources and influence. But how many *Fortune* 500 firms can you name? Suppose you stopped 100 people on the street and showed them the *Fortune* list. How many could identify the principal products or services offered by individual companies?

There is a somewhat perverse reality concerning large organizations and the media. Although corporate giants, unions, government and other institutions receive extensive press attention, one can argue that general media coverage is remarkably limited considering the players involved.

Suppose General Widget, a $5 billion conglomerate with 32 factories in 11 states, increases sales by 12 percent. A news release goes out, but what gets into print? Maybe a paragraph or two in business sections or just a single line in a list of corporate earnings. What gets on radio or TV? Five seconds on a business report or maybe nothing.

What's the problem?

Large organizations often have little to offer to reporters other than size. They've grown big over many years doing things that in many cases are not new ("We built the Cloverdale Works in 1903"), innovative ("We've been making the #407 widget for 36 years now") or particularly understandable to the nonspecialist reader, viewer or listener ("The reverse camber rod flexes inversely when the glombar decelerates, causing the rear fleenstones to twist laterally").

There are many General Widgets in the world and they often compete for attention in a limited number of national media outlets. With so much competition and so little space, it's obvious that not everyone will receive coverage.

Besides, if a large entity is covered by the national press or seems likely to receive coverage, then local, regional and specialized media may feel the story has been pre-empted by coverage elsewhere.

General Widget—with its excellent information program and media contacts—is always there. A journalist who cannot find information and ideas from other sources can always go back to a General Widget.

Individuals and small organizations, however, are rarely beset by the problems above. Being small often means being new, innovative and highly competitive. There may be similar companies or organizations elsewhere, but relative to a given area or industry a small firm can be unique. National outlets are not likely to scoop local media, and massive, ongoing media marketing efforts are rare among individuals and small entities.

Small businesses are often at the heart of terrific stories. Would you rather read about companies closing and factories laying off workers or about new technologies and prosperous entrepreneurs? Small organizations must be doing something right. According to the *President's Report on The State of Small Business,* small firms added 2.65 million new jobs to the work force between 1981 and 1982. Large companies, those with more than 500 employees, accounted for a decline of 1.7 million positions.

The media, for its part, would love to hear from more individuals and small organizations. But for journalists, the problem of dealing with individuals and small businesses is that it's hard to tell who represents a good story and who doesn't. There may be 5000 small organizations in an area or industry, but do reporters really have the time to call each one?

If you're an individual or have a small business, you might want to help those periodicals and stations that might *reasonably* have an interest in you or your ideas, products or services. It's okay to send a brief letter to a few journalists, something that says, "If it ever happens that you do a story about my product (or service or industry or whatever), we may be able to provide information (or a plant tour, statistics, reports, a lively interview, and so on). We've been in the business for 14 years (or, 'We've developed a new technology,' or, 'I'm the president of an industry group,' or, 'We're the largest seller of widgets'), and we may be a useful source when it comes time to develop a story. Please feel free to call."

Given a choice between calling old sources time and again, or new sources who may offer different perspectives, journalists will be open to new contacts. After all, the very fact that there is a new source may justify or validate an otherwise mundane story in a business always looking for something original and different.

8

PRINCIPLES AND PROTOCOLS:
The Rules for Media Marketing

Every profession and industry has a particular way of doing things, a series of standards and approaches that distinguish "insiders" from the rest of the world. If you're in the field, you know where the boundaries are, what constitutes professionally appropriate behavior and where corners can be cut.

In the relationship between journalists and promoters there are also a variety of unwritten, yet observable, understandings to follow if productive marketing programs are to evolve. These caveats can be divided into three major groups: "yeas," "nays" and "cautions."

"Yeas" are actions, or non-actions, entirely acceptable within journalism. No one will be offended if you write a letter proposing a story idea, even if the idea isn't usable.

"Nays" are taboos, steps to avoid if you want either credibility or coverage. Including $100 bills with a news release may assure media attention, but it's not likely to be the kind of attention one might enjoy.

The third category of behavior, "cautions," represents situations where there are no universally accepted norms. You need to act thoughtfully in such cases, because it's entirely possible to needlessly offend someone if you don't.

For instance, suppose you and a journalist have lunch: Who pays? You? The reporter? Do you share the bill? The answer may depend on who invited whom, the journalist's comfort level with you, the topics discussed and where the meeting is held. The answer may also depend on the reporter's employer. Some news organizations have no rules on the subject, while others strictly limit business lunches and other matters, not because they think reporters will be corrupted, but because they worry that such meetings may create a perception of impropriety or obligation.

If the bill comes and you're unsure how it should be handled, it's always fair to say, "I'll be happy to pick up the tab, but I know some organizations have rules about luncheons. Would it be better for us to split the bill? You tell me what's best." Now the issue has been recognized and the reporter can comfortably suggest a solution.

Here, in brief, are a variety of yeas, nays and cautions to consider.

PROMOTIONAL YEAS

To the extent possible, tailor your efforts to individual reporters and media outlets. All media outlets, even those competing in the same field or for the same audience, have distinct needs and interests. An idea unacceptable at one outlet may be a lead story elsewhere. The bad news is that because media interests differ, a single, universal pitch sent to hundreds of media outlets will have a very low rate of success.

Reporters can only allocate a limited amount of time to consider various story ideas, so why should a journalist display great enthusiasm for a proposal sent to vast armies of reporters? Journalism is a tough, competitive business and reporters earn no medals duplicating coverage. If your story is important, if you want maximum consideration, customize your proposal for each outlet and reporter you contact.

The idea of customizing materials may seem tedious and time-consuming, so the question often arises, Should every story idea be customized? The answer depends on the subject's importance. The more important to you, the more customizing is in order. The less important, the more appropriate to churn out standardized news releases (and the less likely they'll receive serious attention). If your company has just named a new vice-president, that event could rate individual contacts to several relevant media outlets. If the company has 200 vice-presidents, the news value isn't great and so a simple release will be appropriate, as will minimal coverage.

Journalists are forever in the position of making judgments, trying to decide what's important and what isn't. If you want media attention, if you believe something is significant, then you need to spend time thinking about the needs of individual reporters and media outlets. If a story idea only rates a standardized news release, you've so much as said your "news" isn't especially important. If it were, then surely you'd take the time to say why. In effect, deciding whether or not to customize materials strongly influences editorial judgments.

When appropriate, send more than a news release. There are often ideas which cannot be adequately explored in a single news release. When faced with a complex subject, successful promoters provide supporting materials such as fact sheets that briefly outline story concepts, question-and-answer dialogues to address complex issues that cannot be discussed within the space of a news release, and background statements or histories to give perspective and show why a story is important.

Maintain credibility. The central measure in journalism is credibility, a fragile value which must be upheld in each article or broadcast. A reporter's words and information must be reliable, his or her public must be able to count on what is being written or said.

In a similar fashion, promoters must also be credible. No one will be surprised if you have a point of view or bias— that's expected from promoters. But information presented to the media must be *truthful,* complete and in context, standards which apply to news releases as well as interviews and supporting documents.

Build perception. In the battle for media turf, perception can be as important as reality. And perception—like bridges and dams—can be engineered.

When the President's Commission on Organized Crime issued a report favoring widespread drug testing by urinalysis for government employees there was considerable debate. No one, explained proponents, would want an air traffic controller to land planes while under the influence of drugs. Those who opposed the idea said it was unworkable, unconstitutional, unreliable and a gross invasion of privacy.

Whatever the merits of either view, proponents lost an important battle when one of their leaders was surprised in public. At a congressional hearing filled with reporters and television cameras, a top commission staffer was asked to submit not only his words, but also vital fluids—in the presence of a witness, just as government employees might be required to do under the commission's proposal. The bureaucrat refused and the undeniable public perception was clear: If a top commission staffer wouldn't agree to a surprise drug test, why should anyone else?

Become a source. As journalists gain experience they develop a network of regular sources on whom they rely for information, ideas and opinions. Such sources may be quoted in print or on the air, but in many cases they supply information on a "background" basis; that is, without public attribution. Many associations, for example, make researchers, specialists and librarians available to reporters on a background basis.

Initially, it may seem as though not getting public recognition defeats the entire purpose of promotion. After all, isn't the idea of media marketing to generate media exposure? But being a source is important for several reasons.

First, if you're a source, you're credible. A journalist won't bother calling if you're not reliable.

Second, as a source, you're influential. The reason a reporter calls is because a story is not complete. For some reason more information, ideas and perspectives are needed, and whatever you provide can affect the ultimate content and context of a story.

Third, when seeking coverage, sources have direct entry to the media since they're at least familiar to journalists and have proved reliable in the past.

Be aware of deadlines. Journalism is a time-sensitive industry with such products as the 6 P.M. news, the morning paper and the December magazine.

Formulate campaigns so media outlets will have enough time to consider and possibly cover your story. If you're aiming for March magazine coverage and the publications you want to reach are assigning stories for that issue in November and December of the prior year, it's easy to see that advance planning is necessary.

Time sensitivity is another aspect of deadline awareness. If a daily reporter has a 3 P.M. deadline, don't even think of a 2 P.M. chitchat. Not only won't the conversation be lengthy, but future contacts are likely to be chilled.

Identify other sources. Few stories have just one side and reporters will want a variety of viewpoints to balance the features they write or broadcast. If you've got the names, addresses and phone numbers of people who might make good sources, that can be valuable information to pass on to a reporter, particularly if some of your sources are competitors or oppose your views.

It may seem as though the idea of identifying alternative sources defeats the purpose of media marketing. Why should you help someone else receive press coverage, especially a competitor or opponent?

One reason is that a story will have greater value, and thus a better chance of being used, if it has balance. Another reason is that an enterprising journalist will speak to a variety of sources anyway, so why not provide names and numbers up front? A third reason is that without conflict there may not be a story. Who cares if three people agree that, yes sir, it'll sure snow in Maine this winter. Find someone who argues that it won't and you have the beginning of an interesting story.

Have perspective. There are products which can objectively be described as "new" and "improved," but how many are utterly perfect? How many times is there only one approach to a given problem?

If your story concept is good, if your idea is compelling, then it should be open to discussion and criticism. Not only does open debate make for a better story, but it also demonstrates an essential strength, character and dimension that makes something, or someone, newsworthy and credible.

As an actual example, in the early 1970s a small manufacturer developed a new method of making contact lenses. With the use of a laser, tiny holes could be placed in a contact lens. These holes allowed greater volumes of oxygen to reach the cornea than regular hard lenses. The lenses were valuable for certain patients because with more oxygen reaching the cornea, some would be able to wear their lenses longer and in greater comfort.

In developing a media strategy, the company wrote a history showing the evolution of contact lenses dating back to da Vinci. It had a one-page news release that announced the new lens, but the release very carefully stated that while the lenses benefited certain patients, they were not valuable for all. The only way individuals could determine if the lenses were right for them was to see an "eye-care professional." This approach produced several interesting results.

First, because the company freely admitted the lenses were not the most wonderful invention since Ben Franklin's bifocals, it had credibility.

Second, the company did not want to be in the position of creating false hopes for people with acute eye problems. Its conservative posture, its willingness to acknowledge the limitations of its product, gave it credibility.

Third, few reporters knew the history of contact lenses or that da Vinci is widely regarded as their inventor. The history gave perspective and dimension to the story, made it something more than just a health products feature.

Fourth, by telling people to consult with individual "eye-care professionals" the company accomplished two goals. It properly sent prospective patients to optometrists, opticians and ophthalmologists for individual attention. It also avoided being aligned with either optometrists, opticians or ophthalmologists, three groups which sometimes compete for the same patients.

Fifth, those very same eye-care professionals mentioned by the firm were happy to receive referrals through the news media, a fact often noted when they ordered lenses from the manufacturer.

Correct mistakes. People make mistakes. Organizations make mistakes. Journalists make mistakes. Mistakes being entirely common, why not say so?

Journalists do not expect the people they interview to have the linguistic fluidity of an Oxford don. Reporters want accuracy and they recognize that a media interview is not a pop quiz.

Interviews can make people nervous and nervous people can forget information, invert words or ramble with something less than their usual coherence. If you find that in the midst of an interview you goofed, say so. If the interview is finished and you realize a mistake was made, call back the reporter as quickly as possible. Print copy can often be corrected before it goes to press, and radio tapes can also be edited in many cases, but the situation with TV is more difficult. It's unlikely that a TV station will send out a camera crew twice or that an interview program will have a second "take" once taping is finished. At best, hope that errant TV material can be cut.

Name a contact. In large organizations there should be one central office or media-wise person to expedite press inquiries, arrange interviews and locate information. This is a common arrangement for mid-size and large-size corporations, associations and governmental agencies.

Many business, civic and social groups, however, handle media relations by naming their president as the media contact. This is a "benefit" of leadership (if you enjoy the spotlight), but as a practice it assumes that organizational leaders can speak knowledgeably to the media. There are often problems when the president, being president, tries to deal with all the media inquiries received by the group. For instance, a local lawyers' organization may be headed by a patent attorney. Since he's president, he answers all media questions, but what if the inquiry concerns local divorce rules? Or, what happens if the attorney is a terrific legal scholar but a lousy interview?

An alternative for groups is to develop an expertise list. Poll the membership, find out who's interested in what, make up a roster with several names under each heading and then distribute the list to the media. The very fact that there is such a list may suggest story ideas and new contacts.

Maintain press contacts if something goes wrong. Groups and individuals in the news are often remarkably accessible until problems arise. Then, suddenly, people aren't in, calls aren't returned, and folks who once burned up the phone lines looking for coverage disappear.

The "take to the hills" response to bad news cedes all promotional ground to one's adversaries and critics. There's no possibility of defending your position or explaining what went wrong. Every group, corporation and organization needs a crisis-management plan and part of that plan must include a willingness to speak with the media.

The 1982 Tylenol poisonings in Chicago illustrate the best way to handle an emergency. Here, in an actual example, a lunatic had laced drug capsules with cyanide and several people died. In full view of the public, the manufacturer removed capsules nationwide from store shelves and took back capsules purchased by consumers. The cost to the company may have been as high as $250 million, a staggering expense. But not much later Tylenol was back in the market as a best-selling painkiller. The public saw that the manufacturer had acted fairly and quickly, that it was willing to take tremendous losses to protect its customers and that in a sense it too was a victim. A marketplace catastrophe was turned around, in large measure by the manufacturer's willingness to deal openly with a terrible problem and by the widespread sense of trust which followed as a result.

Assume you're on the record. Unless you have a clear agreement to the contrary, whenever you speak with a journalist assume that your name and information will be used in a story.

Feedback is important. With feedback, whether positive or negative, a journalist can decide whether to continue coverage of a given subject, change his or her approach or drop the matter completely. If you receive coverage, wait a few days and then tell the reporter what happened because of the story with a quick phone call or a brief letter. Feedback is not only valuable for reporters, it's also important for promoters, a way to stay in touch that's not contrived, artificial or adversarial.

PROMOTIONAL NAYS

Avoid blanket mailings. Sending releases, for example, to six reporters at the same news outlet at the same time in the hopes of coverage by each can be a disaster. In the worst possible case, each reporter will develop a story, the stories will be printed on the same day in different sections of the paper and you will never again appear on the pages of that publication.

Don't socialize excessively. Journalism is a business and while there are times when it's appropriate to socialize with reporters, such moments are limited. Certainly promoters should not call reporters to talk about the weather or gossip as a way to induce media coverage.

Don't relate advertising to editorial coverage. The purchase of advertising is a marketing decision that should be made on the ability of a publication or station to reach a particular audience at a given cost. Conversely, advertising alone should not be a bar to editorial coverage.

While some media outlets *do* relate advertising to what they call editorial coverage, it's clear that the most desirable publications and programs do not. The value of editorial coverage is based on credibility and there isn't much that's credible when ties with advertisers are obvious and overt. If you're going to contact reporters associated with independent media outlets, forget about advertising. At best, the subject places an unhealthy pall over any contacts you may develop; at worst—and most likely—your conversation will end abruptly.

PROMOTIONAL CAUTIONS

Don't expect journalists to be your promoters. Except for advocacy forums such as editorials and signed columns, a journalist's only obligation in news stories and broadcasts is to present information and ideas to a given public fairly, accurately and in context.

Don't believe that friendship is a substitute for a poor story. Rather than relying on personal relations with a reporter, editor or broadcaster to pitch a story, good promoters stress news values such as how a story will benefit the journalist's audience. Suggesting that a story should be used merely because a reporter is a neighbor, buddy or golfing partner demeans the journalist's integrity.

Avoid promotional excesses. The most important promotional inducement is simply information. Meals, tours, samples, trips, and so on must be viewed as possibly inappropriate and handled with extreme care.

Is a luncheon or sample excessive in a given promotional effort, or is a favor expected in return? For instance, if a reporter is going to be at the plant all day, proposing lunch on-site or nearby seems reasonable. Driving 150 miles to the most expensive place in the state is inappropriate.

There are some businesses and activities where the line between appropriate and inappropriate promotion is very hard to draw. If you're in the cruise business and you have a new ship, is it appropriate to suggest a story? Sure. Is it appropriate to pay for a reporter's room and board? That's not so clear. Some publications and stations will allow such arrangements, others will not. Those banning free trips will pay the full retail cost if they elect to do the story.

What if you have a steel mill. Is it appropriate to give a reporter who tours the plant a quarter-pound test casting drawn directly from the flow of molten iron? Why not? After all, the lump has little, if any, monetary value and it does demonstrate how molten iron is gathered for testing purposes. In the context of finding out how steel is made, it seems difficult to imagine that a reporter could be unduly influenced by such a token.

Note, however, there are absolutists in the fourth estate who seriously worry about such galactic issues as free key fobs and complimentary pens. The principle of journalists receiving goods of any value, not the tokens themselves, is a source of conflict. Yet somehow, magically, no one seems compromised by preferential postal rates for publications, the free use of space and facilities in government buildings or the inherent value of all those spokesmen (and spokeswomen) and news releases that are the basis of so many stories and which, in effect, represent an undeniable form of subsidy.

Because the issue of promotional items and services is so sensitive, because feelings are strong, promoters should tread carefully in this area. Always question if something of value—lunch, a token, a ride to the factory, whatever—is clearly related to a story. If not, forget it.

Avoid invective. It's easy to say things in conversation which look awful in print or sound terrible on the air. Because you can't control the arena where your remarks will appear, a good interview rule is, be circumspect. You may feel a competitor is missing a few chromosomes, but save that thought for private moments. Keep disagreements factual and concentrate on why your case is strong, not how your opponent's view is weak.

There are no guarantees in media marketing. The best efforts to promote a story can fail for reasons wholly outside the promoter's control. A story can be bumped to make room for another item or because an editor simply doesn't like the topic, the writing, the reporter's approach or a hundred other reasons.

Do the principles and protocols described in this chapter *guarantee* media coverage? Not at all. But it seems difficult to believe that one could follow these guidelines and not maximize such media attention as a story may deserve.

9
TEN WAYS TO KILL A STORY

With so many publications and broadcast stations looking for good stories, you'd think most promoters would have little trouble getting ideas into print or on the air. Yet many valid story concepts are never covered for the oddest of reasons: The promoter prevents coverage! It happens more frequently than anyone might believe but there are practices which make even the most intriguing story excruciatingly difficult to develop. And the result is that reporters move on to friendlier possibilities. Here are ten quick situations where promoters kill their own stories.

1. A firm's media contact has good relations with local reporters, but management refuses to give him straight information about the company. Journalists bypass the company because its spokesman is not privy to the data they need. Guess who's fired, says management, because he can't get the firm's name in print?

2. When reporters want information about Colossal Clam Industries all they need do is call Wanda Insight, the All-Knowing, Centralized Font of Bivalve Knowledge, a virtual encyclopedia of clam-shell news, prices, trends and history. But what happens when Insight is out to lunch, in a meeting, on leave or traveling? Can anyone else talk about the firm's sales in the past two years? "No," says Insight's assistant, "it's against company policy. Only Ms. Insight can speak to the media." When will she be in? "Next Tuesday. Maybe." You have to wonder how the company will survive if Insight is

ever hit by a bus. Do reporters, unable to catch the illusive Ms. Insight, continue to call?

3. A reporter has just spoken with the company president, Mr. Mumbles, who is interesting, informative and quotable. Later the firm's media whiz calls to ask if more information is needed. Hearing of a particular topic, the reporter is told, "You can't write about that subject. Mr. Mumbles had no right to discuss that with you." Really? How did Mumbles become president?

4. A news release is sent to reporters marked "Copyright 1988 Invisible Management, Inc. All rights reserved. No part of this document may be quoted, reproduced or stored in whole or in part without the express written permission of Invisible Management, Inc." Does this mean a reporter must ask permission to use a news release? Do you think many reporters will bother calling when other stories await?

5. The phone rings and a voice asks, "Is Reporter Thompkins there? Could you hold for Mr. H. Pickford Pickford, president of Pickford Industries and a man so important he uses the same name twice?" Is Mr. Pickford unable to dial, an invalid? Is there an unsubtle hint that Mr. Pickford's time is more precious than that of the reporter? Do reporters enjoy such intimations?

6. Williams contacts magazine writer Bell with a story and promises not to say anything to other reporters until Bell's piece appears in print. Later, Bell is chagrined to see "his" story in the morning paper. Does Bell ever call Williams again?

7. The Pristine Pines Ecological Paving and Concrete Company schedules a news conference to announce a new method of cobblestone extraction. After the firm's president reads a statement he says, "There's no sense in asking questions, all the information you need is in your news kits," and walks away from the podium. Will you read about Pristine Pines in the morning paper?

8. Since the first apes climbed down from their primordial trees, mankind has sought relief from the humble hangnail. So when Dr. Vernon Brilliant walked into a local newspaper office to announce a cure, there was more than mild interest. When asked for supporting studies, documentation and peer reviews, however, Dr. Brilliant was long on explanations and short on paper. Can reporters cover unsupported medical breakthroughs?

9. After meeting for lunch at LaDeduction, Sedgewick the entrepreneur told a reporter for a local TV station that he hoped their conversation would result in a story. So the reporter would not forget, Sedgewick made a point of having his secretary call the station each day to remind the reporter of their conversation. When, after six weeks, no story was aired Sedgewick wrote a bombastic letter to the broadcaster which included a copy of the luncheon bill. Was the reporter pleased by such attention?

10. Reporter Franklin was compiling a chart of two-bedroom condominium units in the area. He called each of 200 projects, explained what he was doing and asked three simple questions: Do you have two-bedroom units, are any now available and how are they priced? At the Shacks of Swampmead, the agent told Franklin she would be happy to give the information he sought, but only if he visited the model homes and watched a two-hour video presentation. Guess why the chart was titled "Selected Metro Condos" and the Shacks of Swampmead was somehow missing.

10

HOW TO HIRE A PRO

Media marketing has become a major business with academic degrees, professional associations, high-priced specialists and a level of sophistication rivaling such studies as marketing and business administration. Yet despite the professionalism which marks its best practitioners, media marketing is not a closed vocation with a jealous priesthood holding back knowledge. With study, observation, and common sense, most of us can successfully adopt media marketing concepts for our own use and thereby gain the benefits of media coverage. Whether one chooses to use a pro or do-it-yourself, the point remains that either selection may be feasible, particularly for individuals and small organizations.

But which is the better choice? There are arguments on both sides of the question.

THE CASE FOR HIRING A PROFESSIONAL

Check the Yellow Pages (under "Public Relations Counselors") and you can find vast numbers of people and organizations providing every possible media marketing service. But how do you select from such lengthy lists? What criteria are appropriate?

Selecting a media marketing professional is much like choosing a lawyer, doctor or accountant. There is more to consider than simple measures such as years in the business or academic degrees. Media marketing is a highly creative endeavor where chemistry and rapport are important and where no single provider, no matter how able, is right for every client.

The critical measure in media marketing is performance, the ability to create positive distinctions, work well with clients and execute programs within budgetary constraints. Private practitioners and firms of every size can be competitive in a field where ideas take precedence over hardware, square footage and lengthy employee rosters.

Media marketing is more art than science, and the ability to generate constructive, usable ideas is crucial. Being creative does not necessarily require the expenditure of vast sums of money, nor is a big budget in itself a substitute for creativity. Consumer groups, with few promotional dollars, are often masters at promotion even though they may have limited financial resources. Beware of media marketing counselors who suggest the equivalent of spending $81,000 to open a hot dog stand when you might do better by simply giving out free samples.

Regardless of your project, there are certain basic issues to consider when looking for media marketing services.

Is the individual or firm inventive? There's no shortage of dull promoters, so find people with a demonstrated ability to create distinction and dimension. When you look at their work, is it clever? Credible? Something that parallels your needs?

Is the firm or individual interested in what you're doing? Some professionals specialize in given fields, such as financial services or retail sales, and they may not want to deal with political candidates, product development, or whatever.

Is your account of sufficient size to maintain the firm's interest? If not, do you want to be a small account with a big company, or is it better to be a large account with a small firm or individual practitioner? Realistically, do you have a choice? In the real world it takes a certain number of dollars to justify projects with larger firms.

Is the firm or individual so overwhelmed by current clients that their ability to take on new work is limited? In such an environment, it's tough to be creative and give the level of service clients should expect.

Does the firm or individual now serve clients with whom you compete? Practitioners will not normally take on competing clients because of the potential for conflict. For instance, if two construction companies are clients and the practitioner has one dandy promotional concept, which company gets it? Which retailer is called if a journalist wants a single interview?

Who will do the work? With large firms, work such as graphics, typesetting, writing and media relations is likely to be handled by in-house staff. With an individual or small firm, part of a project will probably be contracted out to specialists. Neither approach is universally better, or worse, than the other.

What about press experience? There are individuals and firms without press or broadcast experience who offer excellent media marketing services, but no one denies that a media background is advantageous. Former journalists should know how their business works and how to place stories. Conversely, media experience by itself does not insure coverage. A former reporter may know a lot about journalism but very little about promotion. Also, his or her experience may be too focused; that is, a client may need help with newspapers, but a former reporter may have only TV experience, or vice versa. The bottom line: If the choice is between two otherwise equal professionals, media experience is a definite edge.

What about related experience? If a practitioner has done promotion in your field, that can be a plus for two reasons. First, the experienced individual probably has established contacts with media outlets that are important to your program. Second, you don't have to educate him or her about your business; someone else already paid for their training.

What should it cost? Fees for media marketing services are negotiable and practitioners can be hired at an hourly rate, for a specific project or on a monthly retainer that's a credit against fees for services performed. In addition, media marketing experts often receive an override for such expenses as printing, mailing, and other costs incurred in the course of a marketing campaign.

Monthly retainer agreements are frequently used but often misunderstood. The problem is that because practitioners are paid each month, clients feel there should be a major monthly activity. Too often the demand for monthly performance leads to shallow promotional efforts which only devalue a client's overall program. A better approach is to review performance quarterly or by the project.

How can I choose between competing professionals? Media marketing specialists meet prospective clients through personal contacts, advertising and sometimes even through media coverage. Once a contact is made, the client usually receives a proposal which explains what the firm or individual will do, how it will be done, how long it will take and what it will cost.

Proposals, however, cannot be too specific. If prospective clients received an in-depth analysis of their communication problems plus a point-by-point series of solutions, complete with wording, artwork and documentation, then the media pro's services wouldn't be needed. Pros try to offer a fine balance, suggesting how they would approach a problem without giving the client enough material to do it alone.

From your perspective, if someone can't take the time to write a decent proposal, or if they can't communicate their ideas well, it's wise to seek alternative assistance.

Can I get guaranteed results? Beware of promoters who promise the world ("Sure, work with us and you'll be right on the cover of *Time*"). Ethical, rational professionals can only promise to make a credible effort, to use their skills fully and to work in good faith. They want your business and to do less would be foolish, to promise more would be ridiculous.

THE CASE FOR DOING-IT-YOURSELF

One of the most attractive aspects of media marketing is its democratic nature. While there are many pros in the field, there's always room for newcomers with fresh ideas. You don't need a license, there's no entrance fee and media marketing is not restricted to those with advanced degrees or twenty years of training.

Another attraction is price. It can be far less expensive to go the do-it-yourself route than to hire a professional. However, "less expensive" does not mean "free." You need to consider the value of your time and the fact that it's likely to take a lot longer for you to do the things professionals quickly accomplish. If you're a physician and earn $100 an hour, paying $50 for an established pro can be a bargain. If you make $5 an hour, doing-it-yourself may not be an option.

Can you do it? Many promoters can, and many promoters have, especially individuals and those involved with small organizations.

There's no better way to receive a media marketing education than to go out and devise your own promotional package, prepare materials, contact reporters and see what happens. But if going solo seems too hard or inconvenient, then try a mixed approach: Do some of the work yourself and hire a professional on an hourly or project basis for the rest.

You can obtain help in many areas, from creating strategies to writing news releases, and if some portion of your program is too technical or difficult, the pro is there to do the work. A mixed approach offers something to both the promoter and the pro. You gain access to professional services as you need them. The pro acquires an opportunity to work with you, demonstrate skills, and get paid. Presumably, as your program grows, so will opportunities for the professional.

PART TWO

CONTACTING THE MEDIA

Central to every media marketing program is direct contact with reporters. To reach a given public you must first interest reporters in your story.

But how do you begin this process? How do you reach journalists? In the section that follows we'll not only explore how to contact reporters, we'll also examine how to find the right journalists and media for your needs and even how reporters can find you.

11

ANSWERING JOURNALISM'S
FIVE QUESTIONS

The most important period in the media marketing process occurs when programs and strategies are first developed. Getting in print and on the air may be both profitable and productive, but the odds of getting media coverage are limited unless journalism's five basic questions can be answered.

Media marketing programs evolve because we all have self-interests. Our desires may include more sales, higher profits and greater recognition, goals we can often obtain or enhance through positive media coverage.

Journalists, however, have a different perspective. Their interest is not in how promoters benefit, but how readers, viewers and listeners are aided by a given story. To test the validity of a story idea, to see if something or someone is newsworthy, reporters will ask five basic questions: Who's involved, what happened, where did it take place, when did it or will it occur and why? Here's how these questions might be discussed if a new pottery opens in town.

Who is involved? Is it a company, civic organization, governmental agency or individual? Who is affected? Consumers, employees, users or people down the block? A movie star, congressman or the hometown kid who became a success?

Knowing who's involved and who's affected tells you which publics need to be reached. The pottery opening may interest business readers, local residents concerned about traffic and pollution, local residents who look forward to the additional taxes the new plant will generate, publications that follow the industry nationally, people who want to buy at discount directly at the pottery and nearby residents looking for work.

What is the story about? With the pottery opening there may be a major theme ("plant to open") as well as several minor story ideas such as a company history, growth in the pottery industry in general, domestic producers versus foreign pottery manufacturers and how the plant may bring other businesses to town.

Where a story occurs is significant because people relate to one another on the basis of location. We root for the home team, read about our neighbors, listen to area politicians and watch local weather reports. News outlets, in turn, often gear their stories to location. The community newspaper, by definition, will exclude matters that do not affect the neighborhood. The local radio station tells us about commuter tie-ups in our area, but not in distant cities. The largest paper in the state will write about the local pottery opening, but not about a pottery starting in Canada.

When did, or will, the story occur? News is time-sensitive and with the pottery opening we have several deadlines. The first official firing will be arranged with newspaper and television deadlines in mind. If the local paper has a 3:30 P.M. deadline, the opening ceremonies may be held at 10 A.M. —an hour chosen to allow reporters enough time to attend the event and finish their stories well before any deadlines.

The pottery opening lends itself to less time-sensitive feature treatments as well. There are pre-opening stories ("Pottery Seeks New Workers"), post-opening stories ("Town Pottery Welcomes One Million Visitors in Eight Months") and follow-up stories ("One Year Later: Town Pottery Judged 'Good Neighbor,' Survey Shows"). These stories have a time sequence, but if one isn't used today it can be published or aired tomorrow with little problem.

Why something is important gives reporters an opportunity to evaluate a story concept. Our pottery opening may interest the public because it's a local story or because the manufacturing of pottery is an ancient and interesting art. If the plant is completely mechanized, then the story might be intriguing because automation is a new twist in pottery production.

Although the five major questions posed by journalists should be viewed as important to promoters, they should not be seen as inclusive. The interests of promoters and reporters are different; journalists have their questions and you should have yours.

For instance, how much time, energy and money are you willing to expend on promotional activities? Is there any way publicity can hurt you? Will competitors, for example, be able to see news coverage and discover trade secrets? What happens if your promotional efforts fail?

What is most notable about promotional planning is how often initial presumptions and approaches are tossed out when viewed through the questions journalists will ask. What happens is not that self-interest is eliminated, but that self-interest is channeled in productive directions. Here are actual examples:

• An association wanted its members included under federal insurance legislation and wanted the media to support its position. But why, it was asked, should members be included? A variety of answers followed, almost all of which fell in the category of self-interest, a not unfair or unreasonable viewpoint. However, when people began to think how patients could benefit, an entirely different set of ideas emerged and a far more *salable* program evolved.

• A group of medical professionals was offered the opportunity to automate their office with equipment that could greatly speed patient evaluations. The technology was terrific and once installed it could lead to considerable local news coverage. But despite these advantages, the high-tech route was ultimately rejected. Why? Because the value of professional services would be in doubt if they could be duplicated by a machine. The machine's very efficiency was a problem. Speedy exams would produce higher patient volumes, but less time would be available to talk with patients on an individualized basis. And talking with patients, communicating back and forth, was a valued quality to these practitioners. Here it was decided that the best approach to promotion was to stick with a proven program of personal communication.

• A major corporation wanted an institutional brochure to discuss company products, plants and services. But what made this company different from competitors who also had nice products, big plants and offered similar services? What differences would interest prospective clients? It took two weeks to outline definable answers, but the company found a far stronger self-identity and produced an effective brochure as a result.

12

HOW TO WRITE SUCCESSFUL NEWS RELEASES

Journalism has its five standard questions and promoters have a standard response: the basic news release. Although a news release should be seen as _nothing more than a brief communication alerting reporters to a possible story_, the concept has grown to the point where news releases are today shrouded in mythology, misunderstanding and mystique.

News releases are misunderstood because lurking between the visible words one can often find a host of unwritten assumptions. It's these expectations, rather than material in the releases themselves, that often sour relationships between journalists and promoters.

False Assumption 1: News releases equal news.

News releases may sometimes be news, but in all circumstances they're tools designed to influence media coverage. The mere existence of a news release does not insure it's accurate, in context, factual or complete. The central problem here is that we would each like to define how we are seen by the world and so a news release reflects our self-perceptions. News, however, requires a range of perspectives rather than a promoter's solitary viewpoint.

False Assumption 2: A news release is successful when it's aired or reprinted verbatim.

If one has a very limited sense of "victory," then perhaps getting a release reprinted or aired is a success of sorts. The difficulty is this: If a publication or station uses your material verbatim, how credible is the rest of their "news"? If credibility is limited, how valuable is the victory?

Suppose a news release says, "Colossal Industries earned $2.3 billion in the last year." Could a journalist just air or reprint this statement on faith in a news story?

To use this release verbatim assumes it's true and, in effect, that the journalist believes it's true. But even if the material is correct, it still could not be used in its present form. The problem is attribution.

If the statement from Colossal Industries is used verbatim, a reader, listener or viewer will believe the words are those of a journalist. This difficulty can be easily resolved by saying, "Colossal Industries reported sales of $2.3 billion in the last year." Now we at least know it's the company claiming sales and not the reporter attesting to the firm's figures.

It's possible to have news releases reprinted verbatim when they provide for attribution or when their content is largely "data" as in names, dates, places, and so on. A release announcing a new 27th vice-president might qualify.

False Assumption 3: A news release is successful when the information it contains is used by reporters.

Yes—and no. It's surely a good sign when release information appears in the media, but this is not the pinnacle of success. There is a higher goal by which releases should be measured: Is the release so interesting reporters call back to build their own stories?

The idea of media marketing, after all, is not only to obtain coverage, but to receive as much coverage as possible. If a news release sets in motion a series of events that leads to a feature article or lengthy interview, that's a far bigger success than just having a paragraph or two buried in a publication or used for five seconds in the midst of a lengthy broadcast.

False Assumption 4: News releases are useful because they allow promoters to spread material quickly to a large number of journalists.

It's true that news releases can be used to disseminate information widely and with speed. But is this good? Not always.

If 25 reporters receive the same release, the information is hardly exclusive, and some journalists may not bother with the story precisely because of its broad distribution. Newsletters, for example, will hesitate to use information if they feel a general circulation publication has the same material.

False Assumption 5: All news releases are meant for the media.

Some portion of the huge number of news releases received by the media are never intended for publication or broadcast. They are, instead, the products of internal politics, releases sent out because someone with ego (and clout) needs to be mollified or because an itchy client wants *action.* Rather than argue, it's easier to write a release, send it out and then if nothing comes of it, blame reporters. ("Well, we're trying, sir. Just last week we sent out 14 releases, all with your name right there in the very first paragraph, but for some reason we just can't get past those hacks in the media. But don't worry, I've checked the supply room and we've got 41 cases of stationery on hand, enough to churn out 50 or 60 releases a month for the next six years.")

False assumption 6: Journalists can't wait to read the next news release.

Maybe it's the movies or television dramas, but somehow the idea has developed that reporters eagerly arise each day yearning for the latest consignment of releases.

Think about it. Do you enjoy getting mail from people you've never met? Are you thrilled by the prospect of receiving 15 unusable pieces of mail each day? Will your level of delight rise or fall if the number reaches 100 or 200 unwanted releases per day? How will you feel about such a daily influx after six months on the job?

The problem for journalists is that buried within each day's literature may be the seeds of a worthwhile story, so looking through news releases is a necessary chore. And because the mail must be read—or at least skimmed—promoters have a chance to compete for a reporter's time and attention. It's that opportunity which makes the development of a workable release worthwhile.

NEWS RELEASE BASICS

If you shuffle through 100 news releases, the probability is that they will each have an essential similarity. This likeness stems from the idea that with news releases, as with good architecture, form must follow function.

The purpose of a news release is to quickly convey information in a competitive environment. Although it's placement, positioning and utility that "sell" the release, a release will be incomplete, if not useless, without certain "resource" information.

What is resource information and why do you need it?

Go back to the idea of a "successful" release. *A winning release is not merely a handout used verbatim by the media; rather, it's a device designed to stimulate editorial coverage.* If a release is complete, if it contains all the quotes, concepts and ideas anyone, anywhere, will ever want, a journalist has little incentive to look further or to ask questions.

A release that's more than a basic announcement ("Fred Wilson named Manager") should entice reporters. One sure way to encourage inquiries is to produce a delicately balanced release, one that tells enough of a story to generate interest, but not as much as a journalist might want to know.

Since a good release is incomplete, it must say where reporters can find more information. It's these details that comprise the "resource" material found in every good release.

Resource information may seem dull, uninspired and uninspiring, but like a good timetable it has its uses. Here's what you need:

Who sent the release? The individual's name and organization (if any) plus an address should be shown, usually with a logo or in a single-spaced, typewritten block in the upper left-hand corner of the page.

Is there a contact? A name and phone number should be at the top of the page, usually in the upper right-hand corner.

Is there an embargo date? Sometimes news is "embargoed," an expression which says a release time has been established and broadcast or publication is prohibited before that time. Embargoes may be established with a capitalized banner above the body of the release saying: "NOT FOR RELEASE PRIOR TO APRIL 30TH AT 10 A.M. EST."

Embargoes make sense in only the most limited situations. For instance, a magazine may send out a release about a hot new story a week before the latest issue hits the stand. Early distribution may be required to reach media nationwide but advance publication would hurt sales; therefore the publisher establishes a release date and time.

But embargoes should be avoided for several reasons: They may be ignored, they're a barrier to coverage (there's enough news available without waiting for someone's carefully planned release), and a specific release time may hurt some outlets and favor others (morning versus afternoon papers, for example).

A suggestion: Skip fancy embargoes. Just write, in capital letters above the copy, "FOR IMMEDIATE RELEASE," and everyone will be happy.

For whom is the release written? If the copy is single-spaced, it's fairly useless to a reporter or editor because there's no room for editing marks or additions. Always double-space material.

Is it a novel or a blurb? A release should be short; one page is best. If the release must be two pages, use two separate sheets of paper. That way if the material is cut apart by reporters who want to use certain paragraphs, material on the back of the page won't be lost.

How to say you're finished. It's a journalistic tradition to put "- 30 -" at the bottom of news copy because, so the story goes, the first telegraph message was thirty words long. To end the transmission, the telegrapher wrote "30" so the receiver would know how many words were in the message. It's quaint, but it works.

CREATING A NEWS PACKAGE

To some degree the process of attracting media attention can be compared to a multistage rocket; each stage has a particular function, but place the stages in the wrong order and the rocket becomes unworkable. A news release can be seen as the first stage in a promoter's effort to gain media interest, but what works well in stage one is often inappropriate later.

No matter how well-written, informative or interesting, a proper news release is a physically brief document and thus, by definition, its contents are limited. And although the notion of being to the point bodes well when initially competing for a reporter's time and attention, it can also be something of a liability further along in the story selection process.

For journalists, the first efforts to screen story ideas often involve rummaging through bales of letters, releases and phone messages. In this environment brevity is important.

But in the second go-around, when only plausible story ideas are being considered, conditions change. While there are fewer competitors, the competition that remains is far tougher. All the releases and letters say something of interest to the reporter, but not all will result in coverage.

Releases in the second go-around wash out for a variety of reasons. Some are simply less significant than others. Some are victims of poor timing, a condition that often arises for reasons well beyond the promoter's control, such as a heavy news day or conflicting journalistic schedules.

But many releases are unusable for a curious reason: They don't provide supporting documentation. In effect, the brevity that made them attractive in the first sorting causes them to fail in the second.

The solution is to recognize that if you want coverage, then something more than a basic news release is typically required. Rather than a news release, a *news package* is needed, a package that includes both a release and supporting materials to substantiate claims and validate ideas. The news release gets the promoter through the first sorting, while the supporting materials—more extensive and detailed information—clarify issues in the second go-around.

The case for supporting materials and information can be demonstrated in three common situations.

Suppose the reporter is a generalist. He or she may receive 30 wildly different story ideas in a day. Since no one can possibly be an expert in so many fields, it's important to have supporting information to document a story idea.

Alternatively, the reporter may be a specialist, in which case he or she may be an authority in a given area. It's unlikely that a news release will contain enough detail to satisfy a reporter's interest and so more information will be needed.

The third case simply reflects common sense. Journalists are busy people. If they have a choice of two equally valid story concepts and one requires ten hours of research and the other three hours, which concept will be selected?

There are an endless variety of additions that one could plausibly include with a news release. Here, with admittedly elastic definitions, are the most common and useful items to include.

Fact Sheets: In essence a fact sheet is often nothing more than a stark news release, a listing of basic information. For example, if the Tick and Tock Clock Company has just developed a new wristwatch, one that plays Top 40 hits, a news release might discuss the watch and what makes it unique. A fact sheet could describe the company and its size, production facilities, annual sales, work force, other products and industry rank or market share. A second fact sheet (yes, there can be more than one) might look at the watch's technology, how its production is automated, how new songs are added each week, and so on.

Question and Answer Sheets: Q&A sheets are effective because they allow promoters to first frame and then answer selected questions. The information is presented in a format that's easy to absorb and a wide range of subjects can be covered.

Histories: Capsule histories are particularly useful since they provide background and show the relationship between the subject and a given industry, idea, community and so on.

Documents: If your mailing list is either short or selective it can pay to send entire documents such as reports, studies and even books. If you send a document, however, it also pays to mail a brief summary. Anyone who then wants to read the entire document will have it available for study.

Photos: Pictures can supplement a news release if they're black-and-white eight- by ten-inch glossies for newspapers or 35 mm color slides for magazines. Check with local TV stations for individual requirements.

Video Tapes and Audio Cassettes: Often developed by professional producers, tapes and cassettes can be very useful, particularly for electronic media. Beware: Long tapes and cassettes are unlikely to hold someone's interest. Go for eight to ten minutes of material.

Although supporting materials may be costly to assemble and produce, they should never be sent out on a widespread basis with the expectation that they'll be returned. Think about it this way: If a candy company gets your name from a mailing list and unilaterally sends you a box of their latest concoctions, are you required at your expense to send it back?

NEWS RELEASES THAT FAIL

Although the idea of a news release is to generate media attention, the huge proportion of unused releases suggests something is wrong; somehow even promoters who know the mechanical requirements for good releases (names, phone numbers, double spacing, release dates, etc.) are off the track.

How is it possible to create a news release that's unusable even though the subject is potentially newsworthy? Botched news releases, unfortunately, are easy to concoct, particularly when the promoter doesn't understand why a release is imperfect.

Case 1: " 'Federal lawmakers will have to ease tax restrictions on domestic feldspar production if industry capacity is to rise,' according to Homer T. Smith, president of the Obscure Minerals Council."

On its own this release is okay. The difficulty is this: Homer has denuded an entire forest knocking out daily releases for the past five years. Editors receiving envelopes from Homer don't open them because Homer is just not important enough to be a daily feature. The tragedy for Homer is that every so often he says something which deserves coverage.

Case 2: "At a recent convention of all major mechanical testing associations, Lazlo T. Hunzindonger, executive director of the National Coalition for Micrometer Reform, announced that an independent standards-review committee, which will have a major impact on mechanical testing, has been established and is now in effect."

For all the information it conveys, this release may as well be written in a particularly obscure Babylonian dialect. What's the point? Why will the new committee make a difference? From whom or what is it independent? When is "recent"?

Case 3: "Fromqualf Industries announces the introduction of the Fromqualf QUADRAPOWER LASER REAMER, a remarkable improvement on the Fromqualf DYNOPOWER LASER REAMER. The new Fromqualf QUADRAPOWER LASER REAMER will use LASER POWER to vaporize as many as FOUR olive pits SIMULTANEOUSLY, thereby increasing productivity in this KEY FOOD-PROCESSING AREA."

The difficulty here is that Fromqualf has produced nearly unreadable copy because its name is used repeatedly and far too many words are capitalized. Why not rewrite the same information in plain, uncapitalized English and drop a few "Fromqualfs."

Case 4: "The greatest event in computer history will

occur today when King Arthur Computers introduces the amazing, wondrous, labor-saving Round Table #111, a computer that will revolutionize the entire computer industry if not the complete Western World. . . ."

Journalists are constantly bombarded with new idea and product announcements, many hawked in terms that would embarrass P. T. Barnum, were he alive. Reporters tend to view such claims with skepticism, in part because a single day may bring in three "wonders," six "miracles," 14 "marvels" and at least one "awesome."

Case 5: It's 9 A.M. sharp when a delivery truck pulls up with what looks like a carton of lead pipes. But wait! It's not building materials, it's merely a single news release of Olympic proportions; a 26-pounder. Can it be that a reporter will devote an entire day—or week—to reading this massive document? Is it true that the entire release is single-spaced? Can it be there is no cover letter, summary or index? Does anyone believe reporters will use such releases for anything other than door jams, pressing flowers, or ballast?

Case 6: "The Central Club will feature Governor Hern Smith as its guest speaker on . . ." If a release is full of errors, particularly names, journalists—and in this example *Governor Henry Smith*—may wonder about the credibility of both the release and its promoter. At a minimum, a release should be read by several people or checked with a computer spelling program before it's mailed.

HOW TO WIN COVERAGE WITH NEWS RELEASES

Given the various myths, requirements and pitfalls involved, it's little wonder that most news releases fail to generate much attention. Developing a one-page document that tells an interesting story is tough, but the toughest part of all is compressing and encapsulating ideas, concepts and values into two or three leading sentences.

Decisions to read or dump a release are undoubtedly made in the few seconds it takes to scan the first sentences.

If something in those 50 to 100 words doesn't capture the reader, forget it. The rest of the release won't be read (why bother?), nor will fact sheets, histories or anything else.

Having read more than a few releases, it's clear that most fail in the first few words because the wrong points are stressed. Suppose the average family spends $600 a year on gasoline for cars, and suppose further that a company has patented a new carburetor that increases gas mileage by 20 percent. This is an important invention with enormous consequences, and yet so often a release will begin, "Charles Magrew, president of Wesnack Industries, announced today . . ."

Is Mr. Magrew the subject of the release? As a promoter, do you want your fortunes to depend on a Magrew quote?

Winning news releases address two crucial questions up front: What's the point and who's interested? The significant issue above is not that Mr. Magrew is quotable or that his firm has a new invention, but how readers, viewers and listeners will benefit. How much better to say:

> Cars across the country will soon deliver far higher gas mileage than in the past because of a newly patented carburetor that cuts fuel usage by 20 percent. The new device is expected to lower family gasoline costs by $120 a year while dramatically reducing U.S. dependence on foreign oil.

Now we have a release that makes several points in 50 words: Gasoline consumption can be cut with a new invention. Families will save money. Our country will be better off. If you were a reporter (or stockbroker), wouldn't you want to know more?

So now we have an enticing lead. Much has been promised. Let's back it up.

> A patent for a new fuel-efficient carburetor has been granted to Wesnack Industries. The device employs an advanced chamber design which causes fuel to burn more completely. Testing over a two-year period under federal supervision showed gas savings of 14 to 31 percent, with typical users cutting consumption by 20 percent.

From the second paragraph it's easy to see how supporting materials can be developed. What will help reporters?

FIVE BASIC RELEASE QUESTIONS

Releases that lack energy, focus and purpose are common. They reflect the abilities of their authors, devalue their subjects and represent a gross waste of paper, postage and time. Before sending out a release, ask five basic questions:

> 1. Does the release get to the main point immediately?

> 2. Does the release use quotes appropriately?

> 3. Does the release provide a suitable platform for back-up materials?

> 4. Is the release as short as possible, hopefully no more than a single page in length?

> 5. Does the release include all necessary resource information such as contact names, phone numbers and addresses?

• A summary of test results? Absolutely.

• A copy of the patent? It's more theater than information, but it does make the point that a patent was granted, that there is legitimacy to the product.

• The carburetor's history? Go back to the first carburetors and show how they evolved.

• A photo or diagram showing the difference between a typical carburetor chamber and the new design? Yes.

• A background feature on the company? Absolutely. Let's find out who these bright people are.

So now we've created a worthwhile lead and given it some supporting information. What about a human dimension? We could just add another paragraph, but if we put the same information in the form of a quotation from the company president, we may earn more coverage.

Reporters are not hired to reprint releases verbatim in stories, with one major exception: quotations. A quote can be clipped from a release and used directly in a story because it's attributable to the speaker. Therefore, if any part of the release is to survive the newsmaking process intact, it's likely to be a quote.

Knowing how quotes can be used, knowing that the rules for quotes and general prose are different, a promoter can package a release so that certain points are likely to be emphasized in news accounts.

> "We believe the Wesnack carburetor will cut the average family's $600 annual gasoline bill by $120," said Wesnack President Charles Magrew. "In total, the widespread use of this new device should reduce foreign oil imports by 1.5 million barrels a day within five years, a savings to our country of $10.8 billion a year. With less demand, we may see further savings as a result of generally lower oil prices."

Here we've turned from the company and its technology back to family savings and national benefits. A study of consumer gasoline purchases would be a valuable supporting document here, as would a question-and-answer sheet discussing U.S. oil imports.

We could close here but there's a little more room at the bottom of the page, and so another sentence or two is in order. How about a quick cost-benefit analysis?

> Wesnack predicts that its new product can be installed for $110, a price that typical families will recover through lower gas costs within a year. A Wesnack carburetor used for five years should save a typical family $600 at today's gasoline costs.

If you were a reporter, what stories would you see here? Think of the possibilities: How will this device affect local gasoline sales? Who will install it? Can I buy one today, and

Wesnack Industries   Contact: Bill Smith
225 West Main Street   (301) 555-7000 (Work)
Wesnack, MD 20902   (301) 555-3458 (Home)

FOR IMMEDIATE RELEASE

Cars across the country may soon deliver far higher gas mileage than in the past because of a newly patented carburetor that cuts fuel usage by 20 percent. The new device is expected to lower family gasoline costs by $120 a year while dramatically reducing U.S. dependence on foreign oil.

A patent for a new, fuel-efficient carburetor has been granted to Wesnack Industries. The device employs an advanced chamber design which causes fuel to burn more completely. Testing over a two-year period under federal supervision showed gas savings of 14 to 31 percent, with typical users cutting consumption by 20 percent.

"We believe the Wesnack carburetor will cut the average family's $600 annual gasoline bill by $120," said Wesnack President Charles Magrew. "In total, the widespread use of this new device should reduce foreign oil imports by 1.5 million barrels a day within five years, a savings to our country of $10.8 billion a year. With less demand, we may see further savings as a result of generally lower oil prices."

Wesnack predicts that its new product can be installed for $110, a price that will be recovered within one year by the average family. A Wesnack carburetor used for five years should save a typical family $600 at today's gasoline costs.

- 30 -

if not, when? How will this development affect local service stations, car dealers and consumers in the area?

A well-written release creates interest, inspires questions

and starts a dialogue with the media. If a release doesn't do these things, you may as well save a tree, save postage and save a reporter the time it takes to toss out still another unusable release.

13
A NEWS RELEASE ALTERNATIVE

There's little doubt that the simple news release is the single most common form of promotion. Releases are so common it's tough to write one that stands out, but even if someone creates an interesting release, one has to ask, Is a news release the best way to reach the media?

We live in an increasingly streamlined society, one that's computerized, refined, purified and in too many cases sterilized as well. News releases are part of our modern era, a form of mass communication that allows us to reach many reporters quickly and with minimal effort. In a word, news releases are "efficient."

Is efficiency appropriate? Are there situations where being efficient is not the best strategy?

The ability to quickly move information from one location to another perhaps thousands of miles away is a remarkable feat, particularly in a historical context in which entire centuries have been dominated by messengers, drums, smoke and—who knows—maybe pigeons. Yet although the *means* of communication have been vastly altered by technology, the process of *creating* information remains an art. At some point, a live person must think up a concept, write the words and produce the graphics that make modern communication worthwhile.

There is a fundamental conflict here. Journalists create customized work in an era of mass production. And promoters, for the most part, send standardized materials to journalists—a practice that's the equivalent of mailing a paint-by-the-numbers kit to a fine artist.

The point is not that news releases should be banned (though there is a substantial body of opinion within the journalism community that would probably support such an idea), but rather that instances exist where the use of mass-produced news releases is inappropriate and unproductive.

Why is it wrong to sit down and write a letter to a reporter explaining why a story is worth covering? Since individual media outlets serve different audiences and typically offer a vast array of perspectives, why can't promoters originate separate, customized letters for different journalists, letters that show why a particular subject will interest that reporter's specific readers, listeners or viewers?

I freely confess that the idea of writing individual letters is a time-consuming, expensive proposition, one that greatly resembles work. But there are benefits that should not be overlooked.

In an era emphasizing mass communication, individual contact stands out. A letter writer is not only someone who is literate, but also someone who has invested time, thought and energy to communicate with a specific individual. In response, a journalist is likely to invest his or her time reading such missives, if only because they're so rare.

Although writing individualized letters to journalists is attractive, many promoters are tempted to skip personalization and head for the nearest computer keyboard. Why not meld mailing lists with word-processing wizardry to produce computer-generated correspondence? With a good word-processing program and a letter-quality printer, one can create individually typed letters all day that are correctly spelled, devoid of typos and prepared by devices that do not tire, smoke, go out for lunch or strike. Just as importantly, properly prepared letters are indistinguishable from letters written on word processors and electronic typewriters.

Computerized mailings, when properly done, offer the possibility of personalized letters without the drudgery of manual labor. Yet while computerized mailings are not a bad idea in theory, in practice something is often lost. We've all received the kind of "personalized" letter that says

Dear Mr. Resident:
    Yes, we are sending this personal letter directly
to you, MR. RESIDENT, because we know that green,
healthy lawns are an important part of your life-style.
Certainly you want the RESIDENT property to be the
best-kept yard on the block and so we at Plague's
Lawn Service are now offering for a limited time
only a tested, ten-point program . . .

Writers of letters similar to the missive above apparently
believe that form letters can be magically converted into
personal correspondence through the repeated use of a recipient's name. Nobody wrote to Mr. Resident individually;
his name just popped up on a mailing list, perhaps because
he lives in a certain zip code, subscribes to a particular magazine or belongs to a given association. Surely recipients will
wonder about the credibility of the letter writer's product,
service or idea if the letter itself is nothing more than a
heavy-handed, outright sham.

In like fashion, letters to reporters often abuse computer
technology. It's tempting to lean back, press a button, and
send out 200 identical letters. But when TV correspondents
get letters explaining how a story will benefit "readers," or
city magazines are peppered with identically worded letters
to eight staffers, it's obvious that button pressers are at work.

Using computers to generate personal letters may seem
like a contradiction, but properly employed, computers are
nothing more than glorified, labor-saving typewriters. A
well-written letter is a well-written letter, whether it's produced with a computer or a prehistoric manual typewriter.

The use of computers should be restricted to the mechanical aspects of letter writing such as typing and data.
"Data" includes names, addresses, dates, salutations and return envelopes—all of which can be prepared automatically
without sacrificing individuality.

But the body of a letter is not truly subject to automation,
at least not if we are to obtain our goal of personalized contact. The body must be customized for each reporter and
outlet.

Note, however, that "customized" does not necessarily require entirely new wording or a different approach for each letter. It may be possible to work from several standardized text which can then be modified, say one basic letter for midwest radio hosts and another for magazine writers in Oregon. Each basic letter, in turn, can then be customized for individual recipients.

Computer No-Nos

Although computers can greatly speed the letter-writing process, it's important to avoid an assembly-line look. Here are several tips:

• Do not use form paper that tears at the edges. The tears are visible or can be felt. Either feed individual pages into a letter-quality printer by hand or buy an automatic sheet feeder.

• Do not use a dot matrix printer.

• Do not type a name and address onto a pre-printed form and expect results which pass for personalized correspondence. Invariably the individual characters don't quite match or the colors are somewhat different.

• Type envelopes and letters on the same machine.

• Never use an italic or Old English typeface for correspondence unless you're determined to produce an unreadable document.

• Always use stamps when mailing personalized letters. Postage machines represent efficiency, while stamps, and the effort and inconvenience of attaching them to a letter, suggest individual labor and attention.

As alluring as computerization may appear, the sight of whirling daisy wheels and spinning diskettes should cause promoters to keep their goals in mind. The ultimate purpose of letter writing is not to save time, but to gain coverage. If the choice is between mailing 100 computer-generated letters that look like they came off the same assembly line or mailing one letter written on parchment with a quill pen, practice your penmanship.

There's no reason a personalized letter cannot be mailed with a news release and background materials. Indeed, individualized cover letters will greatly enhance the value of such standardized materials precisely because they customize appeals.

As with news releases generally, no one guarantees writing letters to journalists will result in coverage. But if you were a reporter, which will stand out more: another cookie-cutter, look-alike news release or a letter from someone who made an effort to understand your audience and needs?

14

HOW TO PHONE REPORTERS

In seminars and articles around the country, the latest buzz-word in promotion is "telemarketing," a concept with an undeniable logic: If everyone has a phone then the phone system can be used to reach every home and business. And it follows that if every reporter has a phone, every promoter can call.

In theory, there's nothing wrong with one individual calling reporters. In reality, two major problems arise. First, *one* promoter never calls, dozens phone, and part of a reporter's day is lost as a result. Second, journalists must answer their phones. If reporters don't answer, they may miss important stories.

Calling reporters, then, represents an opportunity for promoters. But too often, as with news releases, calling is both overdone and self-defeating.

It's not that calling reporters is offensive per se, but rather that cold calling is uniquely invasive. If a promoter sends a news release to a newspaper, the release can be read or scanned when time is available. If the phone rings, however, an immediate response is required. Whatever work is in progress will be interrupted, and when reporters are in the midst of developing stories or writing broadcast materials, such interruptions are tough to justify.

Magnifying the irritation quotient is the transparent nature of such calls.

Hello, Mr. West. We're wondering if you got our news release last week.

Hello. When do you think *Nimrod's Journal of Wrestling*, the authoritative monthly review of gore, culture and fine interstate dining establishments, will run more features on rope manufacturers. You know, if it weren't for the ropes, American wrestling might look just like sumo matches.

Worse yet, some phone efforts are less organized than Napoleon's retreat. What can you say when a reporter is called nine times in a month by a single promoter or six times in two days ("Are you sure you're not going to write about the new aquarium at Phil's barber shop")?

Phones make reporters *too* accessible and therefore they need to be used with caution. Promoters have a limited goodwill allowance and no one benefits if it's spent on needless or offensive phone calls. Phoning, then, should be seen as a possible method of communication, but only within limited circumstances.

Promoters should never call, for example, to confirm the arrival or use of a cookie-cutter news release sent to 400 reporters. If a reporter isn't important enough in the eyes of a promoter to receive an individualized letter, then the promoter has not invested enough time or interest to justify a phone call.

But if you have written an individualized letter, if you are contacting just three or four reporters before sending out a news package or if one reporter is crucial to your program, then calling may be acceptable.

The call should be brief. If you want business coverage for a new bakery, your end of the conversation might sound like this:

Mr. Conners? Yes. My name is Mr. Whitman and I have a quick question. We've just started a new line of baking products, the first Aztec pepper pies produced in the city, and we wondered if you would want us to send information about what we're doing. We've been active in town for 12 years, grown steadily and we think that with our new product we may grow substantially in the coming year.

(If the call was to a food editor, the approach might be somewhat different; that is, "Mr. Myles? Yes. My name is Mr. Whitman and I have a quick question. We're now producing the first Aztec pepper pies made locally and we wondered if you would want us to send information about what we're doing. A government study has shown that such pies are high in protein, low in fat and seem to offer positive values as a natural snack food or side dish.")

If the reporter is interested, the response will probably be something along the lines of, "Send the information. I can't promise we'll do the story, but let's see what you've got."

You can now send a cover letter ("When we spoke by phone this morning . . .") with your release and background materials.

Note that in the call above the reporter was never asked if he would write about the baker's product, just if he was interested in receiving more information. Asking a journalist if he, or she, will write about a given topic is the equivalent of obligating the reporter to do the story. Since a writer or broadcaster may not have enough information to make an immediate decision, and since reporters are constantly asked to make commitments, the answer is likely to be "No." There are too many stories with less hassle that can be pursued.

Note also that a brief phone conversation is the oral equivalent of the first few lines of a news release. Know what you're going to say before calling because there's a premium for being brief and to the point. Can you describe in 60 seconds why your story idea will be interesting to readers, listeners or viewers? How about 30 seconds? You have a few seconds, literally, to stimulate interest. It's appropriate in such circumstances to write out your pitch, practice till you get it right, and then call. Never read a pitch over the phone. Fair or unfair, journalists often evaluate public contacts quickly, in part because they receive so many.

Finally, it's worth mentioning that the reporter was offered information, not free product samples, and therefore the conversation was not complicated with potential conflicts or extraneous issues.

There seem to be several protocols to observe if you're going to call reporters.

1. Avoid deadlines. If a reporter has to finish a story by noon, don't call at 11:30.

2. Never use an automatic dialer with a taped message to contact a journalist (or any other human being).

3. Always return calls. Returning calls is a response and not a unilateral communication.

4. Don't call at the beginning of the day (9 A.M. sharp) or at the end (4:51 P.M.). People need their psychic space, some time to get organized, settled and adjusted. Calling in the midst of this process is unsettling.

5. Leave messages. If a secretary or machine answers the phone, say who you are, why you're calling, where you can be reached and when.

6. Be brief. Socialization makes it hard to hang up on people but many reporters have overcome this handicap and will put down the phone if a caller's point is not immediately clear.

7. Leave both work and home numbers when contacting reporters. The newspaper you read on December 26 must have been written Christmas day and to produce that paper it's inevitable some people were called at home. Reporters, particularly those employed by daily newspapers and electronic outlets, often work weekends, nights and holidays, which means access to sources is needed at those times.

8. Don't phone repeatedly after the first call or letter. Reporters know you're out there.

9. If you're calling long distance, don't phone collect. Phoning a reporter is a business deal and the cost of phoning is just one cost of doing business. Note that many news organizations have an 800 number.

Some who read these opinions may feel compelled to disagree and if so, that's fine. But please, if you want to make your sentiments known—just write.

15
FINDING THE RIGHT MEDIA

There's no shortage of possible media targets to write or call. A promoter with enough time and money could probably find several hundred thousand potential contacts, but the names and addresses valid at one moment would undoubtedly be out of date the next. Media contacts are always in flux and while no one knows how many news releases are sent each year to people who changed jobs, retired or died, the postal bills and telephone tabs for such errant messages must rival the gross national debt of several U.N. members.

For promoters the sheer number of media outlets is a major problem. You want up-to-date names and information, but you don't want to spend the next 400 man-years compiling lists. Conversely, you can't have an effective media marketing program if you don't know who to contact.

Fortunately there are many directories and guides which track the media. Here's a list of particularly useful references, including several usually found in local libraries.

Bacon's Publicity Checker ($145). Published yearly with quarterly updates, this two-volume set lists more than 17,000 publications and 50,000 editorial contacts. Bacon also publishes *Media Alerts* ($155 including bimonthly updates), a directory of 1,700 magazine editorial calendars, and *Radio/ TV Directory* ($155 including quarterly updates), which provides listings for network and local news and talk shows, PBS stations and college radio outlets. All are available from Bacon's PR and Media Information Systems, 332 S. Michigan Avenue, Chicago, Illinois 60604; (800) 621-0561; in Illinois (312) 922-2400.

Directory Suggestions

The purpose of Chapters 15, 16 and 17 is to give readers an overview of selected publications and services available to promoters. Please note the following information:

1. As the lawyers say, prices, addresses, phone numbers, content and availability are subject to change without notice.

2. The use of directories for particular purposes may be restricted. It's easy to understand, for example, that publishers wouldn't want someone to merely copy their materials and then produce a competing volume. If you have any question regarding the use of a directory, check first with the publisher.

3. If you need mailing labels, many publishers make them available.

4. If you're buying a directory in the state where it's produced, ask about the sales tax.

5. If you're calling an 800 number in the state where the publisher is located, you may need a statewide 800 number or a local phone number rather than the number found here. Check telephone information for details.

Broadcasting/Cablecasting Yearbook ($90). A massive compilation of electronic broadcast media, this reference includes listings for radio (AM and FM), TV and cable outlets as well as a history of broadcasting, FCC rules and regulations, and information about producers and distributors. Broadcasting Publications, Inc., 1705 DeSales Street N.W., Washington, D.C. 20036; (202) 659-2340.

CPB Public Broadcasting Directory ($5). Published annually, this reference work lists all public radio and television stations by state along with an extensive personnel list at each outlet. Also includes a listing of non-station organizations with interests in public broadcasting. Corporation For Public Broadcasting, 1111 16th Street N.W., Washington, D.C. 20036; (202) 955-5100.

Gale Directory of Publications ($115). Once known as the *Ayer Directory,* this excellent compendium of approximately 22,500 media outlets is arranged by location and includes daily, weekly and semiweekly newspapers, magazines, journals and newsletters. Gale Research, Book Tower, Detroit, Michigan 48226; (800) 223-GALE.

Gebbie Press All in One ($70). A single directory with 22,000 listings for daily and weekly newspapers, radio and TV stations, general and consumer magazines, business papers, trade publications, black press, farm publications and news syndicates. Gebbie Press, P.O. Box 1000, New Paltz, New York 12561; (914) 255-7560.

Larimi Communications. Publishes *Radio Contacts* ($222—covers top 300 markets and includes in-depth information on local, syndicated, network and group programming with contacts and guest requirements), *TV Contacts* ($217—extensive listings for local, network, syndicated and group programs for every major commercial station), *TV News* ($160—covers news operations in depth, including producer names and editorial requirements) and *Cable Contacts Yearbook* ($171—lists local major cable systems nationwide with 5,000 or more subscribers and shows which satellite networks and pay services are available. Also lists public access channels and contacts plus information about independent producers including hosts, staffs, and guest requirements and contacts). Those who buy *Radio Contacts* and *TV Contacts* also receive a monthly newsletter. Users of any of the four publications can call Larimi's research department for a city or station update. Larimi Communications Associates, Ltd., 5 West 37th Street, New York, New York 10018; (212) 819-9310.

Magazine Industry Market Place ($59.95). Lists about 4,000 publications by subject and includes information concerning association and organizational outlets. R. R. Bowker,

245 West 17th Street, New York, New York 10011; (212) 645-9700.

Media News Keys ($100) is a weekly four-page update that goes into a loose-leaf binder and shows media personnel information for radio, TV, magazines and newspapers in 35 to 40 top markets (some markets, such as Dallas–Ft. Worth, San Francisco–Oakland and Minneapolis–St. Paul, are combined). Media News Keys, 40–29 27th Street, Long Island City, New York 11101; (718) 937-3990.

Hudson's Newsletter Directory ($75). A useful and well-organized publication that lists subscription newsletters by subject category, this directory shows addresses, phone numbers, frequency of publication, cost and year founded, as well as the names of editors and publishers. Just as importantly, each publication is coded so that directory readers can tell if the letter will consider press releases on industry news, personnel changes, financial news, product news or photos. In addition, the yearbook also lists publishers with three or more letters (in which case you can often cut down your mailing volume) and publishers by location. The Newsletter Clearinghouse, P.O. Box 311, Rhinebeck, New York 12572; (914) 876-2081.

Oxbridge Directory of Newsletters ($125). Contains information concerning approximately 14,000 subscription and nonsubscription letters. Shows names, addresses, phone numbers, etc. Oxbridge Communications, Inc., 150 Fifth Avenue, New York, New York 10011; (212) 741-0231.

By any standard Washington is the nation's media center and there are at least three solid guides to the capital's press corps.

First, the *Congressional Directory* ($13 in paper, $17 for cloth) contains a listing of reporters accredited with the press galleries of the House and Senate. Here you can find newspaper and magazine reporters, radio and TV journalists and photojournalists. Published by the federal government, this publication is available in virtually all libraries as well as through Government Printing Office bookstores.

Second, many of those who write and broadcast in the capital area do so on a free-lance basis. Washington Independent Writers is an association of free-lancers that includes many experienced, well-connected journalists. The group's membership directory ($15) lists members by name and also has a cross-index by specialty. Washington Independent Writers, 220 Woodward Building, 733 15th Street, N.W., Washington, D.C. 20005; (202) 347-4973.

Third, *Hudson's Washington News Media* ($99) is a comprehensive listing of the Washington press corps, which included nearly 4,000 correspondents in 1986. Purchase price includes three quarterly updates. From Hudson's Directory, P.O. Box 311, Rhinebeck, New York 12572; (914) 876-2081.

Publication mastheads: The most direct method to update media contacts is to check publication mastheads and broadcast credits. In addition to core staff, look for contributing editors and regional staffers who may be more accessible than high-ranking reporters in faraway central offices.

Talk Show Selects. A listing of nearly 1,000 radio talk show hosts, producers and programming executives, with station call letters, addresses and phone numbers. Available in a bound edition (255 pages in 1986, $185), on Rolodex brand cards ($195) and as press-on labels arranged in zipcode order ($175). Broadcast Interview Source, 2500 Wisconsin Avenue, N.W., Washington, D.C. 20007; (202) 333-4904.

Working Press of the Nation. A five-volume reference series which originated over 35 years ago, *WPN* includes personnel listings, deadlines and material-acceptance information. The newspaper directory (Volume 1) has more than 60,000 personnel entries, while the magazine directory (Volume 2) includes trade, professional, farm and industrial publications. Volume 3 is a TV and radio directory with listings that include more than 25,000 local radio programs. Freelance writers and photographers are featured in volume 4, and internal publications produced by various corporations and associations are found in Volume 5. Volumes 1 through 3 are priced together at $215, all five volumes are available for $250 and individual volumes can be ordered for $115 each. National Research Bureau, 310 S. Michigan Avenue, Chicago, Illinois 60604; (312) 663-5580.

16

PROMOTIONAL HELPERS: How to Get Your Message to the Media

The overwhelming majority of all promotions are local affairs where the potential number of contacts is limited. Even in a major metropolitan area, promoters may only find 50 or 100 relevant contacts, a not unmanageable number.

What happens if you have a bigger project, one involving ten cities or a broad array of media outlets? Suppose you're faced with hundreds or even thousands of outlets. The physical process of gathering names and preparing materials will consume enormous amounts of time and money.

One shortcut is to rent mailing lists from directory publishers or from mailing-list brokers (found in the Yellow Pages under "Mailing Lists"). "Renting" is not the same as "buying" and users should be careful to understand the distinction. When you rent a list you normally have the right to use it one time; to prevent duplication, lists are sometimes salted with house names that ultimately go back to the list owner. If the list owner gets several mailings from one rental, there's written, dated evidence that at the very least more rent is due.

Not all lists are available to prospective purchasers. In the mailing-list game, you not only need money, you sometimes need prior approval from a list owner or broker as well. If you want to reach all redheaded, left-handed taxidermists with Babylonian surnames, there may be such a list. However, if the list has been compiled by an organization that views you as a competitor, they have little incentive to rent out their cherished names for just a few cents apiece.

List rentals are normally based on a cost per thousand

names, say, $50 or $75 per thousand labels, and lists may be developed by states, regions, cities, selected zip codes, income, employment, credit card use, car ownership or thousands of other criteria.

An alternative to self-mailings is to use a specialized service that takes your release, develops a distribution list and then sends out the materials. One major service, PR Aids, maintains lists of more than 100,000 writers, editors and broadcasters at more than 25,000 media outlets. These lists, in turn, have been divided into more than 2,500 categories. Contact: PR Aids, 330 West 34th Street, New York, New York 10001; (212) 947-7733.

If you want to reach Capitol Hill and the Washington press corps, consider the Chittenden Press Service. For $55, 450 releases you supply can be delivered to media outlets in the National Press Building, in the Capitol Hill press galleries and other locations. Chittenden also has a congressional messenger service which will hand-deliver releases to receptionists in all congressional offices, a service Chittenden says is faster—and cheaper—than mailing. Chittenden Press Service, 1265 National Press Building, Washington, D.C. 20045; (202) 737-4434.

Another way to send out releases is through the National Press Club. Its press release distribution service will print, stuff, mail or deliver releases to 645 assignment editors and news bureaus. For costs and information contact the Press Release Distribution Service, National Press Club, 14th & F Streets N.W., Washington, D.C. 20045 (202) 662-7515.

In addition to mail or hand delivery, several services will now take news releases and other documents and send them electronically to media offices where connections are located.

Electronic services are attractive because they eliminate paper, postage, envelopes, labels, and delays in the mail. In a matter of minutes your fresh, time-sensitive, hot-off-the-wire materials can be in newsrooms around the country.

Newswires are electronically connected to newspapers, news bureaus, magazines, local TV and radio stations, network newsrooms and business publications. In addition to newsrooms, some services are also tied into investment and research departments at major brokerage houses, pension funds and various data bases. Information may be sent nationwide or to given regions and areas. Firms offering electronic services include Business Wire (37th Floor, 1133 Avenue of the Americas, New York, New York 10036; [800] 221-2462), and PR Newswire (150 East 58th Street, New York, New York 10155; [800] 832-5522).

Another approach to news distribution is offered by the North American Precis Syndicate, an organization that sends materials to the nation's suburban publications which, says NAPS, represent 94 percent of all newspapers and publish more than 100,000 pages a week.

What NAPS sends out is a weekly booklet with 20 or so stories in a photo-ready format complete with columns, headlines and artwork. Such materials may produce from 100 to 400 clippings as well as orders, mail to Congress and other benefits. NAPS also packages materials for radio and television. NAPS, 1025 Vermont Avenue N.W., Washington, D.C. 20005; (202) 347-7300.

With so much material being sent to the media you may wonder if any of it actually gets printed or aired. To answer this question there are clipping services, and Burrelle's is believed to be the largest. Burrelle's says it covers nearly 1,900 daily and Sunday papers, 8,000 weeklies, 6,000 magazines, as well as radio and TV stations in most major markets and all broadcast networks. For prices and coverage contact Burrelle's at 75 East Northfield Road, Livingston, New Jersey 07039; (800) 631-1160.

17
HOW THE MEDIA CAN
FIND YOU

If you think about it logically, it figures that if directories can help promoters find media contacts, then there should be resources to help reporters locate promoters. There are at least three sources reporters use to find story ideas and promoters.

The *Talk Show Guest Directory,* for example, is a fascinating guide with more than two hundred pages divided into a subject index, an alphabetical listing and an advertising section. If a producer wants to put together a show on gun control, for example, organizations for (National Coalition to Ban Handguns) and against (Citizens Committee for the Right to Keep and Bear Arms) are listed, with names, addresses and phone numbers.

For information concerning a *free* listing in the subject index and alphabetical section write to Mr. Mitchell P. Davis, Broadcast Interview Source, Suite 930, 2500 Wisconsin Avenue, N.W., Washington, D.C. 20007; (202) 333-4904. Copies of the directory are $25 each, and ad space, at $95 per quarter page, is also available. The directory has a paid circulation of about 2,500 copies nationwide.

If you've ever heard a radio announcer pep up your day with an unusual—but real—anniversary or celebration, the information probably came from *Chase's Annual Events* ($19.45 for individual copies). If you're preparing a special day or week, this is the place to be announced, a famous guide where your event may appear in the 30,000 copies printed each year. No charge if your listing is published, but send information no later than June 30 to make the following year's issue. Mail details about your day (or week or month) plus names, groups (if any), addresses, contacts and phone numbers to *Chase's Annual Events,* c/o Contemporary Books, 180 North Michigan Avenue, Chicago, Illinois 60601; (312) 782-9181.

Newsmaker Interviews is a monthly subscription service distributed to 138 radio stations nationwide as well as newspapers, television outlets and free-lance writers. Forty-five people and organizations are each covered monthly in 200-word capsule reports. No charge if you're profiled. Provides subscribers with information, access and contacts to many newsmakers, including leading personalities in the Hollywood community. (Base subscription price $40 per month.) Contact: Arthur Levine, President, Newsmaker Interviews, 439 South La Cienega Boulevard, Los Angeles, California 90048; (213) 274-6866.

The publications above are obviously good targets for promoters because such publishers are able to successfully gather information of interest to the media. Considering their cost, currency, purpose and audience, they represent an enticing opportunity to reach numerous media outlets without travel or travail.

PART THREE

ONE-ON-ONE
WITH THE MEDIA

Although an enormous amount of promotional work is done through the mails and by phone, there comes a time, hopefully, when promoters and reporters meet face-to-face.

Meeting reporters, being interviewed, even appearing on radio and TV, is a fairly mundane, low-key proposition, more like a college seminar than a prizefight. It's a chance to communicate on a broader basis than a letter or phone call can allow.

Interviews can be held anytime and at any place, with one reporter or with many, but whatever the circumstances, maintain your credibility. You've worked hard to get an interview; don't blow it with unsupportable claims or unreasonable self-interest. Be circumspect in dress, behavior and words, don't lecture and treat reporters respectfully—in other words, act as you would in any business situation.

18
HOW TO CREATE A SUCCESSFUL NEWS CONFERENCE

"Ladies and gentlemen, the President of the United States."

With those words begins one of our most visible and intriguing American institutions, a presidential news conference, one spectacle certain to dominate the day's news.

Presidential news conferences set a standard that cannot be matched. With the White House as a forum and reporters vying for both seats and presidential recognition, what promoter doesn't envy a president's power to attract news coverage? How wonderful to set a time, pre-empt television schedules and know that members of the fourth estate will fill the room.

From a promoter's perspective, news conferences offer the possibility of dealing with large numbers of reporters at a single time and in a single place. That's efficient, cost-effective and far better than trying to schedule interviews all over town.

But developing a successful news conference isn't easy; it requires all the preparation and thinking needed to build a winning news package, and more.

To start, one has to announce the conference with either a cover letter, news release or formal invitation complete with RSVP notation. With the announcement comes an information package—news releases, question-and-answer sheets, histories, photos, fact sheets and so on. These items define the story, give it perspective and provide background information.

Another way to announce a news conference is over the

local "daybook" or schedule of events run by news wires in larger cities. To list a news conference write or call the day-book editor and see how much advance notice is required.

Creating an effective news package is tough; we already know that most news releases fail to produce much coverage, and asking reporters to attend a news conference is even harder. Since news conferences are so difficult to organize, promoters should ask if one is even necessary before sending out the first invitations. Why call a conference? Is the subject so important that reporters will interrupt their schedules to attend? It's difficult enough to interest journalists in news releases, and with a news conference you're asking them to travel back and forth, attend the event and then consider doing a story. The news value has to be so plain, so obvious, that your invitation doesn't fly right into the dumper with the daily crop of unusable releases.

Is there a time element that makes a news conference necessary? News conferences tend to work well with break-ing stories—an important announcement or a new develop-ment. A story that can wait until tomorrow or next week is likely to get more coverage through individual interviews.

What will reporters learn from a news conference that they can't pull from a news release or individual interview? The possibilities include the demonstration of a new product or technique, the opportunity to question someone who usu-ally isn't in town, or a conference to examine a complex event, such as a report, study or trial.

For a news conference to be successful it must not only be newsworthy, it must also be convenient, properly timed, good theater and carefully prepared.

Convenience: The central purpose of a news conference is to attract media attention not otherwise available through a simple news package, and so it follows that a conference should be arranged to meet the media's needs rather than the promoter's.

To start, you need a reasonably central spot such as a local press club, downtown hotel, private restaurant facility,

On-the-Record or Not On-the-Record

Virtually all information given to journalists should be regarded as "on-the-record," an expression which means a reporter can use material you provide and cite you as a source.

In some situations, however, information may not be "on-the-record."

Information provided "off-the-record" means reporters can't use the material in their stories. Such information may provide leads for journalists, and in this sense "off-the-record" material may have value.

"Background" information consists of material which a reporter may use or quote but without identifying the source. When you read that "a senior adviser to the President" said something, you're reading the fruits of a background interview.

Most reporters avoid anything other than "on-the-record" interviews if possible. Should it happen, however, that you want to provide information on an off-the-record" or "background" basis, be absolutely certain before giving the interview that both you and the reporter agree how the material is to be handled.

corporate board room or country club. Less pedestrian choices include offshore oil rigs, airplanes, laboratories, airfields and yachts. Note that if your conference must be held at an inconvenient location, such as a factory far from town, it pays to charter a bus or limo to transport reporters from a central location.

Wherever the conference is scheduled, it must offer certain amenities. TV crews and news photographers, in particular, often have special needs.

Make sure, for example, that your conference site has adequate electricity. At one Washington news conference a past vice president walked into the room, strong lights from half a dozen television crews went on and every fuse in the place blew. The Secret Service was understandably concerned as the entire room went dark. Other items to check include background lighting (never have a window behind a speaker), handicapped access, sound systems (set microphone levels prior to the conference), film or slide projectors (keep spare bulbs handy and make certain slides are in correct sequence and right-side-up) and background noise (beware of locations near ambulance routes, civil defense sirens and new construction).

Timing: Different media outlets have different deadlines and so it follows that promoters will want to schedule conferences to benefit as many media timetables as possible. Many conferences are scheduled for 10:30 A.M., an hour that's attractive because it works well for most outlets and also offers a natural endpoint: lunch.

Presentation: A news conference can be the ultimate "show-and-tell" performance, an opportunity to take advantage of good visuals, demonstrations, test runs and strong speaking skills. It's okay to offer news and a little "theater," as long as the presentation is responsible, in context and appropriate.

In an actual case, when a small railroad wanted to demonstrate a new automated switching system, it didn't just show a roomful of computer consoles. The company took reporters from a downtown terminal by private railroad car, through its yards and then to the switching center. The 100-year-old car was a unique setting for interviews and a stark contrast to the firm's modernization program. Was the car ride necessary? No. Did it make for a better story? Absolutely. Did it attract reporters? Sure; wouldn't you want to spend a day riding a private rail car?

Preparation: Some promoters believe news conferences should be spontaneous events where speakers just wing answers. This is a gutsy approach, but one totally lacking in common sense. A far better strategy is to set up mock conferences beforehand where speakers are grilled and answers perfected in a less meaningful environment.

Absentees: Be sure to send materials designed for distribution at the conference to those reporters who couldn't attend, along with a transcript of questions and answers raised at the meeting.

THE CASE AGAINST NEWS CONFERENCES

Although news conferences seem like an attractive ploy to draw media interest, in the real world they're often unsuccessful. Check the news desks in any major city and it's probable that dozens of full-blown news conferences are being scheduled every week. It's equally probable that many, if not most, conferences don't draw vast hordes of reporters or produce much coverage.

What's wrong with new conferences? How come they often fail?

The basic problem with news conferences is that many are inappropriate and some actually bar media coverage.

At first it may be difficult to see how a news conference could reduce the impact of a given story, but conferences, by their nature, raise subtle problems.

Journalists are intensely competitive and there's a clear preference for exclusivity and being first. But a news conference is a group affair; there is no exclusivity and everyone gets the same information at the same time. That may be convenient and cost-effective for promoters, but it's not so enticing to reporters.

The idea of a news conference presumes that with adequate notice journalists will arrive at the appointed place and at the proper hour. This presumption exists in a vacuum because promoters can't know what breaking events may conflict with their conference or whether competing—and possibly more interesting—conferences are scheduled for the same time.

One attraction of news releases is that such media calls as may result can be handled on an individual basis. If you flub a reporter's question, there's usually some give-and-take, some possibility of correction or amplification. Just as importantly, a weak answer with one journalist will not damage interviews with other reporters. They'll have separate questions, and if the same difficult matter arises again, perhaps the question can be handled more adroitly the second time around.

With a news conference there's a wholly different environment. Questions beget questions, sometimes because reporters like to demonstrate their knowledge in front of competitors (and sometimes in front of TV cameras). Rather than being a one-on-one, human-to-human interchange, a news conference is more formal, more institutionalized. There's less margin for error, and if a question isn't handled well, it won't be a private matter.

Because news conferences are usually a public affair, packaging stories for individual media outlets is tough. There's no way to keep competing reporters from hearing the same information, or, seen from the reverse perspective, there's no way to divide a story into separate parts that can be used by different journalists.

As for utility, news conferences group journalists together regardless of individual requirements. The magazine reporter and the radio broadcaster (assuming both come) share the same information at the same moment, despite their vastly different professional requirements. Production needs guarantee the broadcaster will produce the story first.

Simply stated, news conferences are inappropriate for many topics and events that might otherwise receive media attention. The opening of a pet shop, for instance, is unlikely to warrant a full-blown briefing, but if the shop owner has interesting ideas about animal rights or carries a stock of exotic animals (or refuses to carry a stock of exotic animals), there may be a story. But whatever story there is, if any, it's probably best developed by meeting one-on-one with reporters.

19
RADIO INTERVIEWS

With more than 10,000 radio stations throughout the country, it's not surprising that radio talk-show hosts and producers are eternally looking for guests to capture audience minds, hearts and ratings—preferably at the expense of other stations. Indeed, given competitive demands and vast amounts of time to fill, it's easy to argue that of all the media, radio presents the most opportunities for coverage.

Getting on radio talk shows is a straightforward process: Call the station, ask how guests are booked and then send out individualized letters to each booker with a news release and background materials.

What should the letter say? It should identify you and your credentials, but more importantly, it should package an idea in terms that will interest a given audience.

For example, psychology is a talk-show staple, and a social worker might suggest a program discussing "interpersonal relationships among family members at holiday times."

Ugh!

Real people don't use such convoluted language, but the topic has potential. Why not repackage it in terms that can generate greater interest?

> Dear Mr. Host:
>   When the family gets together at Thanksgiving, is something wrong? Do you find that time spent with Uncle Ned or Aunt Fran is less enjoyable than it should be?
>   Many people feel this way because family gatherings are often not what they seem. Genealogy

may be shared, but not necessarily interests,
life-styles or values. There's pressure to compete
(Does younger cousin Willy make more than you?),
pressure to perform (Still not married?), anxiety
(Have you gotten a new job yet?) and often
embarrassment as well (Remember when George was
a teenager?).

As an experienced social worker with an
extensive private practice, I'd like to talk about how
to take the sting out of family gatherings, how to
make them less tense and more enjoyable. It's a topic
that affects everyone and I'm certain your listeners
would be greatly interested. Tell me what you think.

The mere fact that you've sent a coherent package of
materials to a station should create interest. What usually
happens next is that someone from the station, such as a host
or producer, calls to find out more about you and your subject. They'll listen to your answers and try to gauge your
guest potential. Do you answer questions directly without a
lot of rhetorical mush? Do you use jargon? Can you explain
complex ideas in a simple manner? Do you use examples that
relate to listeners? In effect, the conversation is an audition,
and if you "pass" you'll get booked.

Before appearing on a show it pays to turn on the program for several days and hear how the host deals with
guests. Is the conversation friendly? Abusive? Do listeners
call in? How much air time does each guest receive? Are
there many interruptions for commercials, news breaks and
traffic reports? What topics does the host seem to favor?
Breaking news? Features? Fluff?

Once on the air you'll discover that radio is an especially
wonderful medium because, unlike good children, guests are
heard but not seen. There's an opportunity to "appear" in
public and yet still preserve one's privacy. No one cares what
you wear or how you look.

Usually you'll wind up sharing a table in a small room
with a host, and in this setting it's okay to bring papers and
books and spread them out for reference. A caution: Some

stations allow smoking and coffee in studios, others don't. Ask what the policy is. A second caution: Don't move microphones or make noises. Radio equipment is sensitive and tapping the table or touching a microphone creates sounds that can be picked up.

A common radio format is the call-in show where John and Mary Public have a chance to air their views. The host serves as a kind of moderator between the guest and the listeners, introducing the topic and then taking calls.

Most stations check callers before they're allowed on the air, merely to see if the questions are relevant. When callers are not screened, however, questions out of left field are entirely possible: You're discussing fall fashions and the caller wants to know if the stock market will rise next year.

Call-in shows are great for promoters because they allow immediate interaction with the public. You raise an idea, listeners respond. They raise an idea, you respond. The questions themselves can be seen as a kind of community opinion poll, one that's admittedly skewed by frequent callers and zealots, but a poll which nevertheless gives some idea of what people think. After doing a few call-in shows, you can sense listener interests just from their questions and comments and prepare for future programs accordingly.

From the listener's perspective, call-in shows are attractive not only because they allow participation, but because callers participate anonymously. While guests are identified, a caller named "Don of Closter" or "Mary from San Ramon" could be anyone.

Calls need to be handled diplomatically. Disagreement is okay, berating listeners is not. One good tack is to reverse roles and question listeners; this gives callers a platform to explain their ideas more fully. Some callers have a very clear agenda and use radio talk shows to pontificate, recruit, vilify or propagate. Others raise subjects which must be handled with caution. For instance:

> Isn't it true that the Democrats (or Republicans or Whigs or whoever) lied about taxes last year?

This is an assertion posed as a question. The caller wants your agreement, not your opinion. Once you answer, whatever you answer, the caller will then say, "Yes, but isn't it true . . ." After one or two "Yes, buts" you'll need to change callers or the show will stall: "Okay, obviously you have an opinion, why don't we see what other listeners think."

> Could you predict interest levels (or stock prices, baseball standings, wheat futures, etc.) for next June?

Being a talk-show guest makes you an authority figure and some listeners therefore feel you should know everything. There are two approaches to questions worthy of a soothsayer. If you're not coming back to town, if you think people will forget your answer or if you're indeed a gifted seer, then pick a number. Your guess is as good as anyone's. A second choice is to try humor. "Well, I've been predicting interest rates for more than 20 years and in all that time I've never been wrong. Basically, I believe interest rates will change. Whether they go up or down is not clear."

Your success as a radio guest will depend largely on how well you interact with the host. Recognize that it's the host's show, his or her territory, audience and format. Most hosts are intelligent and personable, friendly people, and you'll get along well with most of them if you're merely prepared and straightforward.

Some hosts, however, will not win contests for congeniality or charm. There are the "sharks" who regard guests the same way wild dogs view raw meat. Regardless of your ideas or positions they'll roast you on the air. More deadly still are the "chameleons," hosts who are delightful off the air but instantaneously turn into snarling interrogators once the mikes go on. After a warm conversation before the show, you may wonder if the host has a twin elsewhere in the building.

The "common man" is another type of host. Rather than preparing questions about you or your subject, the host simply engages in conversation. This can work well when the host is broadly knowledgeable, but the show will break down quickly if your host is woefully ignorant of the topic. Try to help the host and you'll both look better.

If you do well in radio there's often a bonus: You stay on longer. Hosts will frequently say, "We've scheduled you for an hour but if we get a lot of calls, could you stay longer?" Translation: "I'll let you hang around if you pep up my audience."

Because radio is an oral medium it's entirely possible to do live shows away from the station. If you're a successful guest, a host may suggest (or you might propose) future programs by telephone. So-called phoners, or phone feeds, allow you to do shows in distant cities without leaving home, a great way to save time and travel costs. If you do phoners on a regular basis, however, you may develop a good case of "telephone arm," a problem that can be neatly resolved with the purchase of an operator-style microphone and headset. Speaker phones, however, should be avoided because too often they give a hollow, distant tone that sounds terrible on radio.

It's tough to arrange phone feeds if you haven't been on a program or station at least once, but there are several ways to raise the idea.

Certainly it pays to write to hosts and producers in distant cities. Not only do you want to describe your topic and yourself, you also want to mention your radio experience: "As a frequent guest on many radio programs, I thought . . ." In addition to your letter, you'll want to include a news release, background materials and perhaps an audio tape as well. Rather than just a tape of yourself, send a copy of an actual show. It's realistic and proves you have experience. Before sending copies, however, make sure you have written permission from a host or producer to use the material.

Another approach is to call a host or producer. There are many stations and you could run up a huge phone bill calling each one, but a less expensive strategy is to find stations and programs listed in toll-free, 800 directories. Phone and ask for a copy of the broadcast schedule and staff roster, wait a few days and then call back and ask for a specific host or producer. In timing calls, don't phone while a show is on the air (people are busy), just before a show (the program is being planned and finalized) or immediately after a program leaves the air (hosts and producers usually need some time for themselves). Try an hour before a program or 15 to 30 minutes after a show ends. If someone isn't available, ask when it's convenient to call back.

20
HOW TO GET ON TELEVISION

Millions of Americans spend a large portion of their day before television screens, and so it's little wonder that TV has such influence and power. Yet for television to be successful, if we define "successful" as high ratings and growing ad revenues, TV producers must continually find new and interesting stories, personalities and information or face the prospect of losing both viewers and their jobs.

The search for something interesting to televise is compounded by television's staggering ability to consume information and entertainment. All of Shakespeare's plays, the work of a lifetime, are just a few nights' viewing. Scheherazade, who kept her husband entertained for a thousand and one nights, would have been exhausted by television in a matter of weeks.

Talk shows and news programs are typical targets for promoters. Like radio, you need to check directories and call stations to see who does the booking, most probably people identified as producers, assistant producers, production assistants, talent coordinators, assignment editors or news directors.

TV bookers have no shortage of "talking heads," people who can sit and discuss events, news or whatever. Guests with good visual presentations, however, are in demand.

Part of the trick to obtaining TV coverage, then, is to offer something visual. Riding a llama, exercising on a mat or trying a new product all serve to enliven television. If you can take what you do and give it a visual twist, your chances of TV coverage will be greatly enhanced.

Whatever visual presentation you make must not only illustrate your subject, it must also be brief and workable. On a TV talk show with several guests you're likely to have eight minutes of air time to yourself—or less. Visuals must be quick and to the point, so it pays to practice demonstrations before going on the air. Another tack is to prepare part of the demonstration before the show and begin in midstream ("Well, Mary Jo, as you can see we've already got the button weaver started and now we'll show you how to turn those ugly household knickknacks into beautiful buttons anyone in the family can wear").

Ah, but what if you're not going to make the evening news and you don't have a visual presentation? What if you are a talking head, a couch person—can you get TV coverage?

Talk shows are filled with people who sit, speak and do little else. Their attraction is in the words they use, the way they appear and their ideas, opinions and insights. They are, dressed up and polished, the very same people you would want to hear on radio. After all, would you be interested in someone who could help you save money or lose weight? Would you listen to someone who just conducted a poll on the ten biggest battles in marriage or the five best dates?

TV talk shows favor those with visual presentations, but several of the most successful syndicated programs on television feature little more than one or two guests, questions from a host (or hostess) and audience participation. These programs succeed because they ingeniously package subjects in formats that create public interest.

If, as a promoter, you can develop a good talk-show package—a focused topic with a unique approach—your chances of appearing are excellent.

For example, if you have a shoe store, you can't call a TV booker and say you want coverage to increase sales. First, everyone knows that. Second, no one cares. But if you call to suggest a program on the latest styles, or how styles have changed in the past 50 years, or 10 ways to save money buying shoes, you may generate some interest.

Talk-show bookers look for guests who are not only qualified to speak on a given subject, but who are also distinguished by a personal dimension, something in their character that comes across in public. One could argue that successful guests should be urbane sophisticates who exude style, grace, charm and charisma, but how often is this true? Some guests—and some hosts—are rude, combative, abusive and yet eminently interesting. They succeed not because they're seen as role models, but because in a mundane world they add spice, zest and vigor.

Television time is precious, particularly on news programs. If you can get four minutes on a local news program, that's a major success. On network television, few but the president generate more than two minutes of coverage on any given night.

For TV news you need visuals and you need something else: the ability to speak in "20-second bites." Your ideas, arguments and reasons must be compressed into quick phrases that instantly transmit ideas.

For instance, if you're asked why lower mortgage costs are beneficial, don't launch into a detailed discussion of compound interest or loan-amortization schedules. Respond in terms viewers can understand:

> Ask yourself a question. Would you rather shop for the best mortgage in town or pay tens of thousands of dollars in excess interest? Most people don't shop carefully for home financing and the result is that enormous sums of money they might spend on vacations, retirement or college educations is needlessly paid to lenders.

TV assignment editors and assistant producers are always looking for people who communicate ideas quickly and with a flourish. You can't use jargon or define 26 exceptions on the nightly news; there isn't enough time and even if there was, you wouldn't get coverage.

There's a temptation to think that because TV news appearances are short, they're visual bumper stickers devoid of content. This viewpoint is grossly in error. Precisely because news appearances are brief, it's enormously difficult to encapsulate ideas that are factually correct, easy to understand and interesting to viewers. Try this test: Get today's newspapers or a weekly magazine, pick a story, and reduce it to 30 or 40 spoken words.

To obtain TV news coverage, you need to show a viable news angle and a strong visual component. The news angle can be expressed in a letter, news release and background materials, but developing a visual component is often more complex. Sure you can suggest scenes from the factory or an office lobby, but in developing a story proposal remember that programs have few camera crews and their time is extremely limited.

Location and background shots that are close to the station (less travel time) and require little advance preparation are thus preferred over productions that would awe Hollywood. One business network, for instance, routinely has guests on a nationwide talk show and then interviews them later for news broadcasts. Rather than filming at a distant location, the network finds an empty office in its own building and shoots the interview right there. On TV, the setting looks appropriately professional.

BEFORE AIR TIME

To succeed on television you need more than good ideas. Presentation is important, but presentation is often difficult because few people, even those who frequently speak in public, are used to the environment of a TV studio.

Suppose you're a guest on the *Bill Local Show*. You'll be asked to arrive at the station anywhere from 15 to 45 minutes early, a period used for permissions, introductions, attire, reviews and makeup.

Permissions. Most talk shows and many news programs will want you to sign a permission sheet, a statement that gives the show authority to use your name and image for promotional purposes. Such permission statements often

HOW TO PERK UP TV PERFORMANCES

What can you do to enliven TV coverage? Here are six quick strategies.

• Invite the program to do a "remote" from your site. ("We're live today from Wedding World where we're going to see what's new this year for brides and grooms").

• Have a partner. While you talk, someone else can demonstrate a product, dance, cook, exercise, model or create. Your partner provides the visuals but you remain the authority figure.

• Bring samples. ("Well Tom, just for fun we thought you'd like to have the one billionth Cranston's cupcake. We didn't know which flavor is your favorite, so we boxed 100 different samples, everything from chocolate on chocolate to raisin danish strawberry. We'll let you take your choice and then share the rest with the crew and audience. Incidentally, we've also donated 5,000 packages to the shelter for the homeless on McGrue Street and the Police Boys Club on Carter Hill.")

• Involve the audience. ("Could we have somebody come up here and try these new dripless paint brushes?")

• Involve the host. ("Fred, we thought the best way to test our new triple-action seat belt was to arrange a small demonstration. We've set up a car seat . . . .")

• Use examples. Fill your presentation with illustrations that are short, relevant to the audience and understandable. Ask who watches and then tailor examples appropriately.

contain language that makes you legally responsible for slanderous statements.

Introductions. When you arrive at a station someone on

the show's staff will typically greet you in the lobby and then escort you to a "green room" to wait until air time. The green room usually contains newspapers and magazines as well as a large color television so you can monitor whatever is being aired. Here too you can meet other guests. ("Oh, so you're a lawyer defending the civil rights of a gopher. How interesting. And you're on before me.")

Attire. Television is a visual medium and you need a proper wardrobe. Avoid white (it glares on camera) and provocative or unseemly clothes—aside from being inappropriate, they devalue your position as an authority figure. Good dress is commonly equated with good thinking, though obviously there need not be a positive correlation between the two. Test yourself; if two people are talking about gold futures, who are you more likely to believe, someone in conventional attire or someone who shows up wearing a toga and scuba gear?

Reviews. Once in the green room (which rarely—if ever—is green), someone from the show will come and describe how the show works, the host's approach, the day's topics, who watches, whether there's a live audience and how the host will introduce you. Sometimes, too, hosts will drop by to say hello and thank you for coming.

The review process is an exchange of important information. This is the point where guests can correct introductions, suggest or refine questions for the host and better understand the host's interests and goals.

Makeup. Adjacent to the green room, typically, is a makeup room, complete with a table, mirror, lights and a makeup person who is there to render you camera-ready. Some guests find the makeup process disturbing because, first, they don't normally wear makeup and it makes them feel self-conscious; second, they wear makeup but prefer their talents to those of the makeup artist; third, they are allergic to makeup (though most studio makeup is designed to avoid allergies); and fourth, they wonder how this stuff comes off before either going back on the street or meeting one's spouse.

The purpose of makeup is to highlight good features while hiding beard lines, bags under the eyes, teenage skin eruptions, dueling scars or whatever. In addition to the usual profusion of creams, powders, talcs, liners and astringents found in most studios, makeup artists often prepare their own custom-made and homegrown solutions and chemicals—including, at one station, an ominous gray aerosol can marked only as "human dulling spray." While I never did find out the precise contents of this can, I was at least able to discover its purpose. It seems that some male guests have expansive and shiny bald pates, and since something must be done to prevent studio lights from reflecting back into the cameras, human dulling spray was born.

In the TV Studio

If there is a single quality that makes television unlike other media encounters, it's the matter of distractions. If you haven't been on television, think of it as a job interview conducted in the middle of a rocket launch. As you speak and attempt to present a positive image, all around floor directors are pointing, technicians are adjusting, cameras are aiming while you sit deep in prayer hoping that each of your answers suggests some glimmer of intelligence.

The good news about television is that once you're on the air, everyone wants you to succeed. If you do well, the show does well. But television is a high-tech marvel and it takes a lot of people, equipment and dollars to make the marvel work. To be successful you've got to follow the lead set by your host and floor directors.

Once you move from the green room to the set you'll be fitted with a microphone, told where to sit or stand and where to face. More complex, however, is what happens after the initial setup.

All your life you've been told to be polite and face people when you speak to them, but suddenly you may be in an environment where you're asked to speak to your host while looking elsewhere. "Elsewhere" is a camera that doesn't give cues or responses. You're talking, but the camera doesn't blink, shake its head or laugh.

A studio audience largely eliminates the response problem. You can see or sense a reaction to your words. But in a studio without a live audience, the lack of response can be unsettling because the customary clues by which we measure personal communication are missing.

Worse still are situations where you're separated from both the host and the studio. You may be seated in a room off the set, placed in front of a camera and asked to answer questions that come in over an earphone. Viewers see both you and the host at the same time, but you see nothing. Again, clues to measure performance are missing.

Studios today typically have three cameras, and where you look is determined by a floor director who points in one direction or another. The floor director's nods, gestures and signals should be clear, but they can also be distracting as you try to answer the host's questions.

When in doubt, or when the floor director's signals are unclear and you're speaking live before 20 million people, talk to the host. It's natural and the control room should be able to find a decent shot, unless you're espousing some cause which infuriates the crew, such as an end to television unions.

Because TV is an unfamiliar environment, practice sessions have become increasingly common. Large corporations often prepare key executives for television with full-scale practice interviews, complete with actual studios, cameras, crews, lights and current or former TV reporters who act as hosts. Organized by specialized commercial services, such sessions duplicate broadcast conditions and provide realistic feedback for would-be media stars.

Less formal—and less costly—is the use of a simple video camera and monitor. With the widespread availability of video equipment, promoters in every income bracket can now practice their television techniques, respond to questions and see how they look and sound on camera. In the best situations, video practice sessions can be organized by TV consultants who show clients how to make stronger and more effective presentations.

21

THE CHANGING WORLD
OF NEWSPAPER COMPETITION

In an era marked by whizzing electrons, cable TV and radio headsets everywhere, it might seem as though newspapers are a communication dinosaur, a fading technology which holds less public interest each day.

Wrong!

About 60 million daily papers are sold, an impressive figure by any standard. Although the number of big cities with competing dailies has declined sharply in the past 40 years, the information industry—of which the daily press is a part—is hardly comatose. We may have fewer competing big dailies, but there's no lack of entertainment weeklies, suburban dailies, city magazines, business journals, foreign-language publications, religious papers and free advertisers—many established in just the past few years.

Thus, daily papers may be the largest players on the local field, but they're hardly the monopoly of which political theorists complain and their turf and territory are far from secure. Hometown Goliaths must produce a viable product each day or lose readers and advertising to more specialized competitors.

To fight today's competition, daily papers are becoming increasingly segmented. Monday business sections are now common as are weekend inserts on Fridays. When there isn't enough advertising to justify a weekly section, irregular supplements are produced for such topics as new cars, resort living and computers.

Not only are papers becoming increasingly segmented, they're becoming regionalized as well. There are suburban sections and midcity editions, each with a somewhat different slant.

What does it mean to promoters?

First, the public still wants its daily paper. Selling 60 million of anything is an achievement.

Second, papers need massive volumes of material to fill the thousands of pages they produce each day. As a comparison, the script for a 30-minute TV newscast can fit comfortably on one or two pages of a daily paper. Because papers need so much material, there are many opportunities for promoters.

Third, nondaily print outlets should not be ignored. Not only can they provide valued coverage, they can also perk the interest of daily writers. A feature that appears in a suburban weekly can often be rewritten for use by a big-city daily.

Fourth, because of segmentation, daily papers are not monolithic enterprises where a story rejected by one writer is doomed forever. A story that doesn't work on the business pages can often be repackaged as a metro feature or style article.

How to Get Newspaper Coverage

The process of obtaining newspaper coverage begins with a careful review of target publications. Which sections are most desirable? Are there particular writers who cover your field? Have competitors received coverage, and if so, how much and what kind?

It's worth going to a library and reading back over past stories. You may find a pattern of coverage; you'll surely find good background material to help build a news package.

In broad terms, promoters will want to contact reporters (who cover breaking news), feature writers (who write longer, less time-sensitive pieces), editors, deputy editors and assignment editors (who assign stories) and columnists (who produce commentaries). If you have a story that can be packaged for the business, metro, food or feature sections, or perhaps even as breaking news for the first section, you may have 20 or 30 potential contacts to consider.

Who gets your first promotional letter?

Pick the section that most interests you and which is *most likely* to provide coverage. Call up, ask who assigns stories and write that person. Or, if there's *one* reporter you feel would be particularly interested, phone him or her to see if a news package is desired (see Chapter 14).

What happens next is uncertain. A daily paper has the capacity to publish material overnight or even in a later edition that day. Sometimes, though, stories languish for days or weeks and then promoters have practical problems that aren't always easy to resolve.

• You've spoken to a writer, found there was interest, sent materials, but heard nothing after three weeks. Do you call? Write again? Contact someone else? There's no universal answer, but if you haven't had a response after several weeks, it's not unfair to call and ask if the writer got the materials and still has interest in the story.

• A feature writer likes your story, gets your news package, interviews you at length, but no story appears for five weeks. Now what? Do you call? Complain? Contact another writer on the same paper? At this point it's fair to call the first reporter. It may be that the story did not work out, an editor didn't like the article, or the editorial calendar is filled for the next month. You *can't* contact another writer until you know the fate of the first story. If you interest another reporter and the first story is published elsewhere in the paper, reporter #2 is going to be more than annoyed. Conversely, if the second reporter writes about you in one section while the feature article is still in storage somewhere, reporter #1 is going to be upset.

• In those few cities where daily papers compete (and sometimes where a city daily competes with suburban papers) there is an unwritten, but very clear, "first-interview" rule. If one paper doesn't get the first interview, it won't write about you. What happens if you're interviewed by one paper, the article is delayed, and so you do a story with a competing paper that's published first? The folks at the first paper may be upset, which is a serious problem, but at some point there needs to be a clause to the first-interview rule, what might be called the "use it quickly and don't sit on it" statute. Under this regulation, reporters invoking the first-interview rule must be prepared to deliver prompt coverage or forfeit their right to exclusivity.

In thinking about local newspaper coverage, daily big-city papers often receive lavish attention while suburban papers are largely ignored. This is a mistake because suburban papers have much to offer. In their own right they're often large and sophisticated publications, and while they may not be the biggest paper in a given market, they do attract strong reader support. After all, in competing with big-city behemoths, suburban papers must provide something of value to readers or go out of business. What suburban papers typically offer is comprehensive localized coverage coupled with area advertising.

The process and procedure for getting suburban coverage parallels the strategy used for major dailies. Find out who assigns stories, who writes them and then contact the right people. Be aware, however, that as papers get smaller, coverage gets more localized. If you can specifically relate your story idea to the geographic area served by a suburban paper, your chances of coverage will greatly improve.

Once you obtain newspaper coverage, a delightful question arises: When should you again seek coverage in the same publication?

Articles, particularly breaking stories, do beget follow-up pieces and it's conceivable you could appear in print the next day. More plausibly, there won't be a follow-up piece and you'll have to search for coverage from another angle or with a different emphasis. When to ask for coverage again will depend on the original article's length and content. If it was a huge feature requiring lots of space and editorial time,

renewed coverage may be six months or a year in the future.
A short piece may limit coverage from one to three months.
Your name buried once in the midst of a major article should
not be regarded as a bar to next day coverage.

22

GENERATING MAGAZINE COVERAGE

Pick any subject, find any viewpoint, and there's sure to be magazine coverage somewhere. Having so many publications means not only that every conceivable topic is covered, but also that promoters have a vast number of forums in which to seek coverage.

To earn magazine coverage one must first identify publications of interest. If you have something new for CB radio, for instance, you'll want to target CB, electronic and automotive publications. But these publications, of which there are dozens, represent only a starting point. In addition, there are trade and technical journals, wholesaler and retailer publications, industry magazines and a huge number of secondary targets, such as *Popular Science* in this case, that may give coverage but are not primarily concerned with CBs. If the product is sufficiently unique, it might even be possible to realistically view the major newsweeklies—*Newsweek, Time* and *U.S. News & World Report*—as promotional targets as well.

Magazines do not offer the immediacy of radio, TV or daily newspapers and that is their strength. Magazines typically have longer deadlines (publication in three months rather than tomorrow), which means they're able to take a different approach to news gathering. (It should be said that with computerized typesetting and satellite transmissions, some weekly news magazines can be written almost overnight. This is not the usual case, however.)

The attraction of long lead times is that you can do much promotional work before your story becomes news. Many magazines, though not all, can be approached months before you're ready to "go" public.

However, as a promoter you may want your story in print by a particular time, say, early December. That may require promotional efforts one, two or three months in advance. But since there are no guarantees, what happens if December rolls around and none of the 42 magazines you contacted print anything? Or what if they print your story in the January edition? Unless you're hot, you may be "bumped" for a more important story or, if ad sales are poor, because the "book's" size is limited.

Although promoters often want coverage by a certain date, one can argue that the long deadlines and variable schedules offered by magazines are ultimately beneficial.

Imagine a situation where every publication and media outlet publishes or airs your story in a single week. This may seem like a terrific accomplishment, but ask yourself a question: What were the three top news stories two weeks ago? Five weeks ago? Do you remember? What happens if the week your story was publicized the country was absorbed with a plane disaster or international crisis? Sure, you've got clippings and videos, but have you maximized promotional opportunities?

Unless you have a one-time event ("Circus comes to town Friday. Be there!"), promotional efforts are most effective over a period of weeks, months and possibly years—an evolutionary process in which magazines fit perfectly. Coverage may be stretched over time, but *a mix of stories in various media is itself an index of credibility.* The promoter who scores big in a single week may have a fad, while the publicist who gets coverage week after week will certainly enjoy greater credibility and more opportunities for success than the seven-day wonder.

Look at almost any magazine and you can quickly see how coverage is typically divided into current events, feature stories, interviews, pictorials, columns of analysis and opinion plus brief updates on a variety of topics, each covered in a single paragraph. Such formula production suggests that promoters should not only direct their attention to certain magazines, but also to specific sections and forms of coverage within each publication.

Few general magazines offer current-events coverage in the sense of breaking news because production deadlines allow radio, TV and newspapers to reach the public more quickly. Specialized journals, however, are themselves often sources of hard news because they thoroughly cover given areas. The *New England Journal of Medicine,* for instance, is constantly in the news because of its front-running health coverage.

Feature stories, in-depth articles that may run for thousands of words, are a magazine staple. These are the long articles in the middle of the "book" and usually promoted on the front cover, the stories that most reflect a publication's ideas, attitudes and interests. Feature stories are hard to develop and therefore magazines, particularly publications that cover specialized fields, are always looking for new ideas.

New feature material can often be made from updated past stories. Most magazines seem to work on a two- or three-year cycle, so a story that ran several years ago may be updated and used again, only this time with new sources and the latest information.

Magazines often feature regular interview sections and coverage here can establish promoters as authority figures. (If you're quoted in a national magazine you must know something, right?) It's not easy for most of us to suggest ourselves as interview subjects, but such gracious offers are unnecessary. Instead what usually happens is that an interview arises as an alternative to feature coverage because it's sometimes easier to cover a topic with a question-and-answer format. In addition, if a subject is sufficiently famous, an interview format creates exclusivity and bragging rights for the publication ("Chairman Mao Back from the Dead, Read His Fascinating Interview Exclusively in the *Crystal Ball Weekly*").

Interview pieces are typically tape-recorded, transcribed and edited, at which point the subject is sent a transcript to review. Reviewing makes great sense, since substance and continuity can be lost when a wide-ranging two-hour interview is boiled down to 1,500 words.

Magazines have a unique capacity to publish photos, and some publications dazzle the eye with their graphics work. If you want your picture used, make sure it's either an eight by ten inch black-and-white glossy or else a 35 mm color slide. Whether you provide pictures or the publication sends over a photographer, the same standards apply: Find interesting locations and backgrounds, look for unique angles and avoid mundane "head" shots best saved for obituary columns.

Magazines often receive information they want to cover with something less than a full-scale story. One approach to such stories is to reduce them to a paragraph or less for a capsule column. Such features are well read because they're short, easy to absorb and to the point. Getting capsule coverage often takes no more than an interesting news release, but a well-written letter to the writer is probably a better bet. If the writer is unknown and the column is called "Capsule Comments" or whatever, just write to "Capsule Editor." It'll get to the right hands.

Magazine columnists, like commentators everywhere, can write about everything and everyone. Other than the limits of libel, there are no guidelines for columnists and it's a mistake to believe that columnists must be fair or impartial. Their job is to present an opinion, a bias, often saying things which cannot or should not be said in news columns or feature articles.

Coverage by columnists is best obtained by the simple expedient of sitting down and writing a letter. Rather than writing about yourself ("Gee, please write about me in your column because I've been in this business for six years") it's best to comment on a subject: "I was interested in your September 1 column which discussed educational efforts in our industry. We don't know if it's the best solution for everyone, but we have a somewhat different training approach: When a new systems engineer joins our firm we pair that individual with one of our veterans. They share office space, have the same hours and work jointly on projects. We find that both benefit because . . ." A columnist not interested in pursuing the topic is likely to use the letter elsewhere or send it over to another writer.

23
INSIDE SUBSCRIPTION NEWSLETTERS

With so much attention given to newspapers, magazines and the electronic media it's easy to overlook subscription newsletters. Newsletters, after all, aren't at your local newsstand, rarely carry advertising and often have circulations of less than several thousand readers. In the context of media outlets reaching millions of people, newsletters *seem* unimportant—at least to the unwary.

And yet it's a mistake to view newsletters lightly. Newsletters are significant, not because they reach a huge audience (although some letters have six-figure subscription levels), but because they're often the fastest and most effective way to reach selected readership groups.

Newsletters rarely carry ads. Editorial copy, usually four to eight tightly written pages, doesn't compete with advertising for reader attention or time, and the physical size and concentrated content of subscription newsletters creates a unique news product. Items appearing in newsletters are read if only because there are few distractions. Similar material in a big-city newspaper or major magazine may be buried and unnoticed amid 100 pages of editorial clutter.

What makes subscription newsletters important is that such publications must have clear editorial merit to survive. A letter that publishes material from last week's paper can be described in one word: defunct.

Not only must newsletters be fresh and original, they must offer one or more additional values as well.

Specialization. By providing information not typically or fully carried by papers and magazines, newsletters are a preferred channel of information, sometimes the only channel, for certain industries, professions and groups. A court suit involving an environmental issue, for example, may not make the papers generally, even though it may be important to certain business interests and environmental organizations. Newsletters serving such fields will fully report the suit and its implications.

Advance information. Newsletters often lure readers with coverage found elsewhere, but found later. The benefit to readers is that by having advance information, they're able to anticipate trends. If you know the Jones Company has made progress with an anti-cancer drug, that's important for competitors, stock analysts, physicians, pharmacists and patients.

Expertise. Subscription newsletters are typically written by reporters with extensive training and experience who cover a single subject. Between their background, concentration and contacts, such writers are authorities within given fields. Moreover, because they're journalists, they have access to information and people who would not normally be available to competitors in a particular area.

Need. You won't find too much in the local paper, but if you want to vacation on a freighter, there's a monthly newsletter on the subject. Often a topic is so specialized that the potential universe of readers could not justify newspaper or magazine support, so newsletters—with their low production costs and ability to specialize—are perfect vehicles to reach small groups such as those who want to follow injection-molding trends, learn more about intellectual-property decisions or keep up with the potato industry.

Exclusivity. A key feature offered or implied by many newsletters is an "inside" perspective, information that will immediately and instantaneously put you at the center of a given field or activity. What's going on, how to save, who to contact, what to expect—all rendered with detail and clarity—are the mainstays of many letters. Exclusivity is not only an objective appeal, it also offers a subjective value as well; after all, who among us doesn't want inside information?

Contacting a newsletter requires nothing more than finding appropriate letters in various directories and then sending a brief letter and background materials to the editor or publisher.

But if contacting newsletters is easy, getting coverage is tough. Newsletters have little space and what they use must not only interest their readers, it must also appear in print before it reaches the general media. Relative to the space available, there's tremendous competition for coverage. Thus, promoters are most likely to succeed if they package their material for each letter they contact and then send it out quickly.

In addition to seeking newsletter coverage, promoters might also consider another tack: self-publishing. If the particular audience you want is sufficiently important, if your story is ongoing and if you need to be in front of a specific audience on a frequent basis, it may make sense to start your own newsletter.

In the megabuck world of modern media the opportunity to own or start a publication or broadcast outlet is largely reserved for the well-heeled. But although existing print and electronic properties in major markets are often worth hundreds of millions of dollars, newsletters remain the one area within journalism where anyone with ideas and a mailing list has the potential to be immediately competitive.

A captive newsletter can be enormously enticing for several reasons.

1. You control the editorial content. Whatever you want in print is written to your requirements.

2. You have a regular forum to reach specific readers.

3. You can extend your forum to others by offering space for guest editorials, free classifieds, salary surveys, a job mart or whatever. Such features provide an element of editorial

validity not otherwise feasible in a publication devoted solely to you and your interests.

4. As a publisher you may be regarded as an authority figure in your field by general-outlet reporters, someone to be interviewed and consulted.

Over time your letter may evolve into an editorial product of such value that you can actually charge subscription fees. Lest this sound uninteresting, consider that successful newsletters probably represent the highest rate of return on investment one can postulate in the media business. Few dollars and little equipment are needed up front, just labor and that most precious of all media commodities: well-packaged ideas.

24
MULTIPLE CHANCES:
Chains, Syndicates and Networks

A large portion of all editorial coverage comes not from local reporters at a given publication or station, but from outside sources such as wire services, syndicates, chains and networks. The large newspaper groups often have their own wire services and central news bureaus, and papers within groups routinely swap stories. Numerous media services serve hundreds of independent papers. In a parallel manner, radio and television stations are often owned by a single corporate entity, and yet they too can plug into a variety of networks, syndications and services.

News services and networks have a profound effect on the news-gathering process. It's very expensive to send a reporter or camera crew to cover a given story, particularly if that same story is already being covered by a service to which the paper or station subscribes. Besides, it's the development of stories not found on the news services or networks that gives local media outlets dimension and distinction.

Although news services have central staffs to generate material, they also have other sources. Many take local stories and revise them for wider publication or broadcast. Alternatively, local reporters take their own stories and send them to a service. And with feature stories the process is often easier, since revision may not be required. A story on auto safety or beating holiday doldrums could run anywhere.

News service time and space, however, are tight. National wire services transmit from 66 to 1,200 words per minute—not a lot of material in the context of news for the entire country.

But even if a story runs on a news service, it must still be selected by local editors. While some will pick out a given story, others will ignore it. Some will take stories and file them for research purposes, while other editors will assign reporters to devise localized articles on the same subjects. Thus news service coverage guarantees widespread distribution, not necessarily publication space or broadcast time.

Suppose Mr. Drover develops $12 computer software that allows children to quickly and easily understand basic math. To promote his creation Drover devises a simple plan: He'll mail out review copies with a cover letter to the media and hope for coverage.

Drover could send copies to the nation's 1,200 TV stations, 10,000 radio stations, 1,700 daily papers, 7,500 weekly papers, 5,000 commercial newsletters, 5,000-plus magazines, and 20,000 association publications. However, Drover—not having been mentioned in the wills of the rich or famous—must limit his marketing effort to 100 media outlets. Which outlets does he choose?

One category, certainly, would include the five or ten leading educational publications, particularly those going to elementary-school math instructors. A second category would encompass newsletters and magazines that serve the computer education and retailing market. Media that serve bookstores generally and children's bookstores in particular would be a third choice.

To this point, Drover has mailed 80 of his 100 precious disks. His approach has been to directly influence educational authorities and retailers, but he also needs to reach end users, or in this case their parents, so he can stimulate public demand.

Drover finds 20 news services, chains and bureaus in various directories and asks for the names of those covering educational or scientific issues. He finds that most services have such specialists and sends each a copy of his program along with a letter, news release and short background paper entitled, "From Fingers to Figures: Math Made Simple."

The competition for news service time and attention is

extremely tough, but Drover has followed a reasonable procedure to gain coverage. He located the services most likely to reach worthwhile outlets. He asked for the right people to contact, prepared separate news packages for each and wrote individual letters.

It's entirely possible that only one of his 20 service contacts will elect to write a story. It's also possible that the one story which is produced will appear in 150 outlets. Thus the fact that chains, news services and networks exist is a big plus not only for local media, but for promoters as well. They create still another media target, one which allows promoters to reach many markets at once and with greatly reduced promotional costs as a result.

25

ADVERTORIALS

A new form of literature has emerged in the past few years, something called an "advertorial." Instead of having independent editorial material surrounded by ads, advertorials are publications or programs where the editorial content is controlled, influenced or actually produced by advertisers.

Whether advertorials should be classified as "advertising" or "media marketing" is a matter of debate. More certain, however, is the idea that properly constructed advertorials offer interesting promotional opportunities.

Advertisers like advertorials because the copy is "safe" (read: uncritical and noncontroversial). No need to worry about investigative reporters; none would work for advertorials. Advertorials are also attractive because they offer a "shopping mall" effect; many competitors in a single place produce more business than competing shops spread over a wide area.

Used as inserts in newspapers and magazines, advertorials commonly focus on such single-subject topics as health, cars and high-tech employment. The sections, which are usually marked as "an advertising supplement to The *Vine Street Gazette*" or—in small type on each page—as "advertising," feature editorial material surrounded by ads. The editorial material may range in content from overt promotional fare (one article per advertiser, or an "editorial" mention for each display ad) to more sophisticated copy that would conceivably fit in regular editorial sections.

TV advertorials are half-hour or hour-length commercials where favored subjects seem to be hair restoration, financial security and instant millions from real estate investments. Some TV advertorials, such as certain wrestling shows, are so popular they even garner sponsors! If there's a heaven for ad agencies it must surely consist of advertisers sponsoring advertisements which are popular with the public. Another approach is the advertorial interview. Here the "guest" is interviewed by a "host" who tells you in great detail how the guest's product, service or book can be ordered. The orders go to an address or phone controlled by the host, who then lops off a percentage of the take before passing the balance to the guest.

Radio advertorials consist of blocks of time usually controlled by a single advertiser. A real estate company might buy an hour of air time each Monday at 3 P.M., or whenever. The company can hire a host, control the show's content, name guests and even run ads on its own program. Unless they happen to catch an oblique announcement ("The views expressed on this program do not necessarily reflect the opinion of this station etc."), radio listeners are often unaware that the program is controlled by the advertiser rather than the station.

Another approach to advertorials is the captive newsletter. While such letters offer "safe" editorial matter, the package of values they provide differs somewhat from other advertorial formats. Captive letters typically have only one sponsor and thus offer exclusivity. Because they're newsletters, they can be quickly and inexpensively produced. Lastly, captive newsletters can be issued on a regular schedule to reinforce messages or on an "as needed" basis for seasonal events.

Although advertorials are attractive promotional vehicles, they're not for everyone. The best advertorials, those offering usable, informative editorial matter, are costly to produce and therefore ad rates are high, a fact which means that not every promoter can participate.

Promoters should consider advertorials from two perspectives. If the advertorial's content is entirely controlled by advertisers, then its potential as a promotional vehicle for non-advertisers is decidedly limited, if not nonexistent. If, however, the advertorial uses solid editorial material, then coverage may be possible, particularly for promoters with messages that coincide with advertiser interests.

To obtain coverage in publications, get a copy of the last advertorial (from advertising departments—don't ask a journalist). See what's written, who wrote it and when the next advertorial is scheduled. Contact the editor and see what stories are planned. Think about the editor's needs and see what you can offer in terms of an interview, photo, diagram, table or other information.

For radio and TV advertorials, your most likely opportunity is to participate in locally produced programs rather than syndicated productions taped in distant cities. Since advertorials have a limited scope, your message must be focused not only toward the audience, but toward the sponsor.

Well-run advertorials constantly seek valid editorial material, if only to upgrade some of the advertiser-induced coverage they must publish or broadcast. It's possible that your subject might be valuable because it adds credibility to the advertorial. That's not a criterion for independent journalism, but then no one suggests that advertorials offer the same values as editorial coverage. Advertorials do offer exposure, however, and the possibility for exposure should not be ignored.

26
HOW TO COMPLAIN

It's hardly surprising that with millions of words published and broadcast each day, some are out of context, not in the best light or simply dead wrong.

There is little doubt that journalists make mistakes. And there is also little doubt that when an error concerns one person or organization, it's supremely important to those affected.

But the problem is that not every "error" is an error. Unlike mathematics, reporting the news is not an objective science. Fifty reporters can attend a presidential news conference and 50 separate stories will result, each with its own nuances and shadings. A magazine with one political or economic leaning may well emphasize an aspect of the conference ignored by a given daily paper. Neither is more "right" than the other, nor more "wrong." Their approaches are simply different.

Yet there are cases where the issue is not merely subjective reporting. The question then becomes: What should be done when an article or broadcast contains objective mistakes, clear misrepresentations or inaccurate quotes.

A gut-level response is often to call or write and upbraid the reporter. This option feels good and offers a certain amount of satisfaction. Unfortunately, it contains a fatal, costly flaw: How will you ever contact the reporter again for another story? A rash action today may preclude coverage tomorrow, especially in a world with a surplus of potential news stories.

A better idea is to consider the problem in context and over time.

1. How serious is the error? Most journalistic mistakes are minimal, inconsequential errors that create little if any damage.

2. Is the story basically correct? If so, do you want to nitpick?

3. Is the error plausible? Could you have given the information or impression found in the story? Is it possible from the way you expressed yourself that a reporter, without malice, simply used your words as you gave them?

4. Were your words correct but out of context? This is a major concern with small snips of material culled from longer interviews. If out of context, just how badly skewed was the material?

5. Did someone in your organization provide material with which you disagree? The problem here is internal rather than with the journalist.

6. Did the reporter use material you felt would not be part of the story, such as statements that were supposed to be off-the-record? Is this situation a misunderstanding or do you feel it's a deliberate breach of trust? Unless you're totally convinced the reporter was "out to get you," chalk it up to a misunderstanding.

If mitigating circumstances seem possible, then it's best to forget the whole incident. However, if you believe the reporter is wrong *and it's important to have a correction,* there are several steps to consider.

• Call the reporter and discuss the problem sanely. Do not question the journalist's motivations, parentage or mental capacity. A better approach is to say, "Bill, I saw your story and felt uncomfortable with one statement. I can't believe I said the earth was flat. Could you check your notes or tapes to see if I really said that? If not, I'd like a correction."

• Write a brief, nonabusive letter to the editor. "In a story published May 7, I was listed as a supporter of those who would close the Middleton School this year. Actually, I want Middleton kept open, as a review of the voting record will show." Unfortunately, there are few realistic letter-to-the-editor parallels for broadcast outlets, but some stations will announce corrections in their own words.

• If the problem is more general, such as the coverage of a group, industry or organization, speak to the editor or—if there is one—the ombudsman. For instance, if a columnist complains constantly about taxi drivers, ask for editorial space or time to offer an opposing view.

• Sue. In our litigious society, everyone sues everybody else, so why not sue the media? Here's why. It's not likely to be productive, the financial costs can be high and if the journalist is right and/or the subject is appealing, it will surely be back in the news again and again. If the issue is embarrassing or upsetting, a lawsuit is one sure way to keep the matter before the public, thus compounding the problem.

Moreover, it should be said that publishers and broadcasters not only don't like to be sued, they'll often countersue as well. One approach which has worked well is to sue attorneys who participate in frivolous libel cases for malicious prosecution. The threat of such suits, which may emerge as an attractive legal tactic in many fields, has undoubtedly deterred much needless litigation.

27
EVALUATION

At some moment in every media marketing program, time must be set aside to consider results: What was accomplished, how could you have done better and what are your next steps?

Evaluation should be used to measure past performance and devise future strategies. Knowing what worked—and what didn't—can be crucially important as new programs are developed. Yet measuring media marketing results is often difficult because the purpose of a given campaign may be expressed in terms which are hard to quantify. How do you measure "an enhanced corporate image" or "better employee morale"?

Even if you can see results through burgeoning sales or surveys which show improved public perceptions, are you measuring the correct issues? How much of your newfound success was a result of your media marketing campaign and how much was caused by factors outside your control, general trends which carried you along?

As an example, one measure of employee morale might be reduced worker separations. If people stay with your firm in higher numbers than before, do you not have evidence that employee morale is on the upswing? Maybe. But what if unemployment rates are generally rising and as a result those with jobs are now holding on, fearing that they might not find employment elsewhere?

More complex still are campaigns which involve the use of both media marketing and paid advertising. You know someone saw your ad if 5,000 coupons are returned. But did they respond because the advertisement itself was innately interesting, or because a receptive environment had been created by your media marketing effort? Given the dollars spent, do 5,000 coupons constitute a good response in any case?

Measuring results is more complicated than looking at raw numbers. Have the right questions been asked? Were the correct people polled? Have the results been interpreted correctly? Analysis and context are no less important than basic data.

If it's at all possible, the best environment in which to measure media marketing results is one without advertising. In an actual case, one medical products firm, for example, had no advertising funds or salesmen. But within its limited budget, the company developed a media marketing campaign that generated coverage in local, national and professional publications. Within a year, sales tripled and the firm moved to larger quarters. Assuming constant demand, there was no factor other than media marketing to account for this sudden growth spurt. Unfortunately, few programs are so easy to measure.

PART FOUR

DEVELOPING MODEL PROGRAMS

Media marketing programs range in size from two-page letters to massive documents not much smaller than community phone books. Regardless of size, however, all programs should first analyze problems and then offer detailed solutions based on media marketing principles.

How does an actual program look? What does it say? The best way to find out is to examine realistic models, and in the section that follows we've outlined programs for a retailer, a professional and an association.

The plans are organized with program elements first and then likely actions and responses. Although the organizations, individuals and specific situations described in the following model programs are entirely fictitious, some elements and wording have been used in actual proposals.

28
PROGRAM I:
Bob's Elm Street Gas & Lube

When we think of retailing we usually envision department stores and hardware chains, yet local service stations are also retail businesses. Small businesses usually run by owner-operators and franchisees, service stations offer essentially identical products and services in a highly competitive environment.

Station profits come from four basic sources: the sale of gasoline, services, supplies and vending items such as sodas, cigarettes and candy. The more you sell, the larger your profits. However, some items are more profitable than others.

Gasoline profits are based on the margin above cost. If gasoline is priced at $1.50 a gallon and the dealer has a $.10 margin, profits will be small. If gas is $.75 a gallon and the margin is still $.10, profits rise because sale volumes increase.

A typical service station has several grades of gasoline, each with a different price and margin. In addition, most stations feature "self-service" and "full-service" pumps, so a single grade of gasoline may have two prices and two margins. Thus the goal is not to just sell large volumes of gasoline (though this is surely desirable), but to sell gas with the highest possible "pool margin price."

Independent stations such as Bob's carry tires, batteries and accessories (TBA) on a consignment basis; that is, the station keeps supplies on hand but only pays for what it uses. This arrangement is convenient (the supplies are there when needed) and economical (no capital is required). TBA markups are typically calculated at cost plus 20 percent or 40 percent of the retail price.

TBA sales, however, are not attractive. Large, single-line retailers who specialize in batteries or tires can offer better prices to the public. Moreover, it takes labor to install batteries and tires, labor which can be more profitably used to service cars.

Servicing—oil changes, brake jobs, tune-ups and the like—are enormously profitable to service stations. Not only is there an opportunity to sell parts, but the station and mechanic typically split labor charges 50/50. Thus a $150 brake job may entail a mere $25 in material costs to the station and produce a gross profit of $62.50.

A final profit center is vending. Although not large when compared to other revenue sources, vending sales require little labor and yield 30 percent mark-ups.

BOB'S PROBLEM

There was a time when Bob was the only gas station on Elm Street, but now two others have moved nearby. Herb's "Jetstream" station sells just gas, but because sale totals are so great, he sells gas at low prices. Bob must match prices to stay competitive, but when he does his margin is so small it doesn't cover rent. Another competitor, "Conlon's Lube and Groove," does nothing but service work and draws many customers who might otherwise come to Bob's.

Bob realizes that to remain competitive, and to profit, he must concentrate in three areas: First, gas sales and pool margins must be increased. Second, the service bays must be filled. Third, Bob's must be distinguished from competitors who largely offer like products and services.

MEDIA PROFILE

Bob serves a small suburban community on the edge of a major metropolitan center. With just one location, he's able to ignore small dailies and weeklies which do not focus on his specific area. His media survey shows four TV stations, 21 radio outlets, one major daily paper, a cable system, 22 suburban papers (of which only four cover Bob's community), one city magazine and two weekly business papers. From his research Bob identifies 41 media contacts.

In addition to identifying media by location, Bob also looks for media outlets that specialize in cars, trucks and servicing. The major daily has a monthly advertorial section for car dealers that consists of ads and soft news ("Clever Ashtray Location Highlights New Phoenician 426"). A public TV station runs a weekly automotive feature, but it's syndicated from out of town and offers no opportunities for Bob.

Without much specialized coverage, Bob decides to use a different approach. He'll package his activities within the realm of "consumer news" and tell how owners can save money, keep cars longer and drive safer.

With many service stations in the area, Bob is unlikely to receive exclusive or extensive coverage. However, whatever coverage is generated will assist in his overall plan to generate more business.

BETTERING THE STATION

Bob's competitors are not only new, their stations are more modern and efficient. To be polite, they're also cleaner. As a first step, Bob must fix up his station. Estimated cost: $5,000 for painting, repairs and upgrades.

The cleanup process begins when several wrecked cars are hauled to the junkyard. Since Bob has his own tow truck, hauling the cars is a simple process. Before each car is taken, however, Bob fills their trunks with old parts and other debris from around the station, thereby reducing his trash-collection bills. In addition:

• The station is repainted inside and out. Even the flagpole is spruced up.

• Bob modernizes his bathrooms with new lights and vanities.

• The waiting area is carpeted and old magazines are thrown out. Bob subscribes to *USA Today,* The *Wall Street Journal,* the local daily, and several weekly news magazines so customers will have something to read in the waiting areas.

• Bob's station, being older, is home to a wide assortment of dead and dying bushes, untrimmed hedges and a forlorn elm tree. He calls the local garden club to ask if they're interested in a project: Bob will pay for seeds, bushes, planters and shrubs if the club will show him how to fix up the station. Club members, who largely regard the station as an eyesore, eagerly accept. The local paper, seeing changes at the station and hearing from club members, runs a feature on the "new" Bob's, complete with "before" and "after" photos.

DEALING WITH THE PUBLIC

Pumping gas does not require a college degree and most stations employ unskilled labor for such tasks. Station attendants should be seen differently: They're the people who communicate with customers. Instead of hiring the first available person at the lowest possible hourly wage, Bob should pay a premium wage for better attendants.

With more money Bob attracts better workers and writes out the rules each attendant is expected to follow:

BOB'S RULES:
THE PROMISE OF GOOD SERVICE

1. The customer comes first.
2. Run, don't walk, saunter or amble, when customers pull into the station.
3. Listen to customers. What do they want? Try to help those with limited mechanical knowledge.
4. Always be courteous. Men are to be addressed as "sir," women as "ma'am" or "Ms." Customers are to be

continued

---

greeted with "Good morning," "Good afternoon" or whatever is appropriate.

5. All customers are entitled to have car windows, headlights and taillights cleaned each time they come to the station.

6. All customers will be asked if they want oil and battery checks.

7. All customer money will be handled with care to assure that proper change is always returned.

8. Mechanics who overcharge or perform unnecessary work will be fired. Old parts, when not used as a credit for new equipment, will be bagged and returned automatically to customers. Customers will be called as soon as work is completed.

9. The station, including bathrooms and waiting areas, shall be cleaned as necessary but not less than twice daily. Trash on or near the station will be picked up immediately.

10. All complaints will be referred to Bob.

Bob likes his rules so much he creates a pamphlet entitled, not surprisingly, "Bob's Rules: The Promise of Good Service." Attendants are required to memorize it and copies are given to customers. In addition, a printer makes poster-sized copies for the waiting room and service bays. Cost for printing and posters: $100.

IMPROVING TBA SALES

Although the markup on TBA sales is attractive, the value of such transactions is reduced because of high labor costs. Bob's should pursue TBA sales which do not involve station labor, such as sales to do-it-yourselfers.

Bob's TBA inventory is maintained on consignment; he pays each Friday for supplies used during the previous week.

To boost sales, Bob compiles a list of local car clubs and teachers who run high-school auto repair classes and sends a letter to each, offering batteries, spark plugs, fan belts and engine hoses at 20 percent off retail prices. The offer is open for one month and in that time Bob sells more than 125 batteries plus other supplies. Since the only labor involved consists of pulling parts from inventory, Bob's effective return is higher than if the materials were installed at the station.

INCREASE SERVICE HOURS

Although the service bays are busy during the day, they're essentially unused at night and on weekends. The station should find activities to employ station facilities during slack times.

Bob places ads in the papers for mechanics to work at night and weekends. He discovers several looking for part-time positions and hires each for one or two nights a week from 5 P.M. to 11 P.M. He also finds someone to work Sundays.

To advertise his new service, Bob gives handbills to each customer and erects a sign announcing his new service. With longer service hours, the station draws people who need their cars during the day. Because the late shift doesn't have access to the range of parts readily available during the day, late-night service is limited to tune-ups, brake jobs and oil changes—all highly profitable work for the station.

With longer service hours, the station is visibly active for a greater span of time. Gas sales rise per hour because, Bob theorizes, more people at the station makes it seem inviting and secure.

CREATE AN OIL BAY

Conlon's draws a steady stream of customers because it offers speedy oil changes, usually 15 minutes or less. Bob's should compete in this field because the station is already equipped to change oil and replace filters, the work requires little technical prowess and, equally important, oil changes are profitable. Estimated cost: $50 for fliers.

Bob designates one service bay for oil changes and hands out fliers to his customers. But since one oil-change service is like another, Bob adds an extra dimension: If it takes longer than 15 minutes after a customer has signed in to change the oil and replace the filter, Bob will pay $1 per minute up to $15. He sends a short news release to the paper and suggests a story on the "Elm Street Oil Wars." No papers are interested. He tries again. This time he drafts a letter to several papers and a TV consumer reporter suggesting they secretly test several service stations and oil-change shops to compare prices and service. About two weeks later an article and chart run in the big-city daily and Bob comes in second. However, since Bob is the only "contestant" from his community, he effectively comes in first because no one else on Elm Street is mentioned.

OFFER ADDITIONAL SERVICES

Gas revenues can be increased by raising sale volumes, having longer hours at the station, shifting the sale mix to more expensive products and attracting more full-service customers. Central to each approach is the need to bring more people into the station. If Bob's is just a gas station, people will only come in for auto-related reasons. If Bob's expands into non-auto-related areas, people who might otherwise not use the station may be attracted. Estimated cost: $150 for fliers.

To pull more people into the station, Bob adopts three strategies.

First, he organizes a waste oil dump, primly named "The Auto Ecology Center." Waste oil—the stuff that comes out of cars and trucks during an oil change—can be a significant pollution source if disposed incorrectly. Bob already collects waste oil from his station for proper disposal; now he offers to accept waste oil from others. He promotes his free service by contacting ecology groups plus fleet owners such as cab companies and delivery services. He also passes out fliers at the station for a week telling customers about his new service. The oil program not only brings in dumpers, but also introduces Bob to several large potential clients. Oh yes, the oil he collects is later sold to a jobber.

Second, "Bob's Buyers Club" is established. Bob hands out blue cards to customers and each time they buy gas, the card is marked by an attendant. For buying 150 gallons, customers are entitled to a free oil change (filter extra). For 1,000 gallons they receive a free tune-up, parts extra. Bob also issues red cards to service customers. Someone getting an oil change gets a free gallon of gas, while a tune-up earns 10 free gallons.

The buyers club concept cross-fertilizes sales. Service customers are encouraged to buy gas (why get just one gallon?) and gas customers are encouraged to have cars serviced at Bob's. The program also does something else: Why pay for an oil change at Conlon's when you can receive one "free" at Bob's? Giving service benefits also helps in the competition with Herb's gas-only station. Herb can't offer service discounts because he doesn't do service work. As for Bob's, oil changes and tune-ups are low-cost premiums that offer solid value to consumers and often lead to additional service work. Estimated cost: none. The additional volume of gas sales and service work negates the additional cost of the premiums.

Third, Bob contacts the county cartography branch and discovers that it produces complete, up-to-date area maps. Not only are the maps available for purchase, but—Bob is told by the chief cartographer—they can be reproduced by county residents under one condition: The maps can't be sold. Bob buys a map and has 5,000 copies printed. He then sends copies to media contacts with a note saying they're free while the supply lasts. Several papers print small notices about the map and one even prints a reduced version. Bob gives 1,000 copies to a local high school and distributes the rest at the station. Bob benefits because the map introduces him to new customers. Estimated cost: about $200 for printing, $15 for postage and stationery.

DEVELOP A REGULAR MEDIA PRESENCE

Since there is little meaningful car coverage, Bob should create his own.

Bob calls the state automobile administration and soon learns how many cars, trucks, drivers and miles of road are located in the metro area. He also calls local industry groups to find yearly sale figures for new and used cars.

Putting this information together, Bob writes to the major daily paper and offers to write a weekly auto column for non-experts entitled, "Hoodlines." He provides statistical data to demonstrate the market's size and potential readership interest, interest which, he points out, could make his column a natural focus for advertisers. In addition, Bob sends in two model columns.

The paper doesn't buy the regular column idea, but an alternative is suggested: Would Bob write a series of ten articles, each dealing with a different topic? If the basic series is successful, perhaps it could be extended.

Bob agrees to the ten columns with one understanding: Following publication all column rights revert back to him. The paper agrees and a letter confirming the arrangement is sent to Bob. Thus Bob not only makes the paper, he also has a source of editorial material for pamphlets and brochures.

Bob's column focuses on such topics as why cabs last so long (the oil is changed every 1,000 to 1,500 miles) and how safety flares should be used. His articles are brief (about 500 words), written from a consumer perspective and each closes with a single sentence saying "Bob Jones, the owner of Bob's Elm Street Gas & Lube, has been involved with auto servicing and repair for more than 20 years."

Bob's articles generate letters and those letters, in turn, become the basis of question-and-answer columns. With letters coming in and advertisers advertising, the paper continues Bob's articles.

Among the paper's readers is the manager of a local radio station who also would like more advertising dollars. He asks if Bob would do a weekly call-in show called "Auto Trend Update." The one-hour program features Bob answering questions and interviewing car company officials, race car drivers who come to town, consumer leaders and state licensure officials. Although not filled with sex or violence, the program draws listeners and attracts ads because Bob speaks in plain English and makes his audience feel comfortable.

Back at the station, reprints of Bob's weekly columns are given to customers. Another flier gives the time and station where Bob can be heard and invites customers to call in. Estimated cost: about $10 a week for printing fliers.

MIDWEEK DISCOUNTS

A review of Bob's records shows that service bays are jammed on Saturdays, Mondays and Fridays; indeed, business is often turned away on those days. Work shifted to midweek times would largely represent additional income because heavy service days will remain busy.

Bob develops a simple plan: midweek discounts. Cars serviced on Tuesdays, Wednesdays and Thursdays receive a five percent discount on parts and labor for all expenses above $20. To promote his plan, Bob gives balloons marked "Lighten Your Bills with Midweek Discounts at Bob's" as customers come into the station. Handing out balloons is hardly a sophisticated approach to promotion, but they're a hit with kids and noticeable to adults. The program results in customers shifting service schedules, thereby leaving more room for service business on busy days.

EVALUATION

Bob's should review projects on a regular basis to see how the program can be amended, refined and expanded.

Bob polls customers for a week and discovers that his effective marketing area has increased and those who use his station tend to do so more frequently than in the past. His pool margins are up, in part because his attendants attract more full-service buyers. His gas volume is larger because of longer hours, his buyers club creates steady customers and the waste oil program introduces him to fleet owners and do-it-yourselfers. In addition, his midweek discounts shift service work to times which were once less productive, and less profitable.

Bob's newspaper and radio work brings business to the station, but most importantly, it gives Bob credibility and a marketing edge that other service stations can't duplicate, even though they offer identical services and similar prices.

29

PROGRAM II:
Building Dr. Gordon's Optometric Practice

Optometrists are primary health-care providers who examine the eyes and visual system, diagnose problems and impairments and then prescribe or provide treatment. Licensed in all states and trained in professional programs requiring four years of postgraduate study, there are about 24,500 practicing doctors of optometry (O.D.s) in the U.S.

Optometrists derive their income from patient examinations and the sale of eyewear. Although only one patient at a time can be seen, eyewear revenues may vary considerably depending on the product sold. For example, a frame with a $20 wholesale cost may retail for $50, while a $40 frame may be marked up to $100. Thus there is a premium for selling more expensive goods such as designer-name frames. At the same time, higher-priced goods tend to be better made and more stylish, important factors for an item with both health-care and vanity-centered values.

Contact lenses are another profit center. Although considerable expertise is required to properly fit hard lenses, the lenses themselves cost practitioners from $12 to $19 apiece for single-vision lenses. Basic soft lenses have a wholesale price of $8 to $25 each while extended-wear soft lenses are priced in the $10 to $35 range.

DR. GORDON'S PROBLEM

Health care is very much a business and optometrists have traditionally competed for patients with opticians and ophthalmologists (M.D.s who specialize in caring for the visual system). Traditional patterns of competition broke up in the 1970s, however, when optometrists were allowed to advertise and large corporations built nationwide eye-care chains. Worse still, at least for independent practitioners, has been the growth of one-stop fitting centers, huge retail stores where patients can walk in, be examined and then pick up glasses made on the premises within an hour. Not only are such outlets fast, but with high-volume and on-site lens production, they also offer low prices.

Dr. Gordon lives and works in a neighborhood just outside the central core of a major city. While his neighborhood has a residential flavor with town houses and high-rise apartment buildings, it's just a few blocks from downtown office towers. An optical supermarket is located in an urban mall several blocks from his office. He also competes with several opticians and ophthalmologists in the area. The ophthalmologists, however, rarely fit glasses or contact lenses except for cataract patients and others with special needs. They often refer patients to Dr. Gordon and in turn, when Dr. Gordon finds patients who need surgical services, he refers them to neighboring ophthalmologists.

For Dr. Gordon, like other optometrists, new trends in eye-care raise serious business issues. Patients don't buy eyeglasses or contact lenses every day, and each sale made by supermarket-style competitors means one less treatment opportunity for independent practitioners. The question for the Dr. Gordons of the world is this: Are they the mom-and-pop grocery stores of the eye-care profession?

MEDIA SURVEY

Dr. Gordon visits the library and quickly produces a media contact list. He doesn't bother with suburban papers, because they don't serve his neighborhood, but he does find two daily papers, six television stations, 31 radio stations, one city magazine, a weekly business paper and an in-town free advertiser distributed in his neighborhood. Both daily papers have weekly "Health" sections and several radio stations feature health-oriented talk shows. His contact list includes 51 names.

EVALUATE CURRENT POSITION

Gordon should first review his business posture. Are there additional steps he can take to find new patients? Is he missing opportunities with his current patients?

Dr. Gordon looks through his files and sees that over 20 years he has examined thousands of patients. Indeed, his files are so voluminous he decides to cull patient rosters and find out which patients are current, and which are not.

He buys a computer and begins to list people by name, address, phone number, date last examined and whether the patient wears eyeglasses, contacts or sports eyewear. The contact lens category is further broken down into single-vision and bifocal patients, those with special lenses, extended-wear users, and patients with either hard or soft lenses. Eyeglass wearers are divided into single-vision and bifocal patients, those with designer frames and those with regular frames.

DEVELOP A BASIC BROCHURE

The availability of low-cost, high-volume, quick-service competitors has a major effect on Gordon's practice. To compete effectively, Dr. Gordon must show that he is not merely a high-priced, slow-moving echo of his newer competitors. Estimated cost: $1,000 to design, write and produce a professional brochure.

Several months after North American Coal, Steel and Eyewear—a major conglomerate composed of 200 corporate subsidiaries—opens a huge retail outlet a few blocks from his office, Gordon notices that appointments are down. The new competitor in the neighborhood has a mall location, frequent advertising, and discount prices. Dr. Gordon is in trouble.

Or is he? A year after North American first establishes its

office, Dr. Gordon notices an interesting phenomenon. Several patients who had gone to the big retailer came back. True, prices were lower, but they didn't know the doctor who served them, and the doctor, they felt, didn't have enough time to know them. North American might be big, but in a service industry it was missing an essential ingredient: personal contact.

With the help of a local ad agency Gordon develops a new office brochure. Called "Who We Are," the pamphlet explains that eye-care is a personal matter and that independent optometrists cared for patients on an individual basis. It also describes what patients should expect in an eye examination, why certain tests are used and the optometrist's role. Although low-key, the brochure emphasizes the idea that professional observation and evaluation were central to good eye-care, and apologizes for the fact that individual exams sometimes took longer than allotted appointments. Unstated, but clear, is the implication that retail outlets might not be so flexible, or so caring.

CREATE A DIRECT MAIL CAMPAIGN

The files assembled over many years constitute a major asset and should be the heart of a direct mail marketing campaign.

With his basic records computerized, Gordon tries a test mailing. Those who have not seen him in five years receive a brief letter asking if they wish to remain current patients or have their records sent to another eyecare professional. ("We are now in the process of updating our files, and we need to know if your valuable examination records should be retained by our office or sent to another eye-care professional. . . .")

Included in the letter is the brochure and a prepaid response card which allows the patient to quickly take two actions. First, the patient can direct Dr. Gordon to forward records to another eye-care provider, maintain them in a current status or toss them out. Second, the patient can direct Dr. Gordon's secretary to call and arrange an appointment. Of 2,800 letters, nearly 1,200 come back undelivered. Records for these individuals are placed in storage. The remaining 1,600 letters result in the return of 480 cards. One hundred and twenty people want records moved, 360 wish to remain current, and of these, 80 ask for appointments.

Dr. Gordon knows that direct mail campaigns typically produce returns of one to two percent and that five percent (80 out of 1,600 delivered letters) is considered a stunning success. How did he generate such a high response level?

• People rarely receive letters from medical professionals, especially letters that ask for advice and input.

• The letter didn't "sell" anything. Nobody was overtly asked to buy a product or service.

• The response card included the recipient's name and address, so to react, it was only necessary to check a few blanks. Little time was required.

• The response card was postage paid. There was no cost to respond and no need to search for postage.

It takes Dr. Gordon several weeks to integrate 80 additional patients into his usual schedule, but their business more than compensates for postage costs, printing and stationery.

Based on his first mailing, Dr. Gordon decides to establish a regular mailing every two months, rotated among specific patient groups. His first mailings go to hard-contact-lens wearers ("Many people have asked about newly introduced extended-wear hard lenses"), soft-lens wearers ("With an average life-span of 12 or 14 months, you may wonder how to tell when it's time for new soft lenses"), and fashion-conscious eyeglass wearers ("We've recently received a large shipment of Parisian Pearl eyewear, widely regarded as the most sophisticated and current eyeglass frames of our time").

DEVELOP A LARGER PRESENCE

Although independent practitioners will not be able to duplicate the extensive advertising outlays of national eye-care retailers, they should at least do promotional work to distinguish themselves from competing optometrists. Dr. Gordon should join with other optometrists to advertise jointly and to share marketing ideas. Estimated cost: $100 per month.

Gordon's advertising options are limited. He can't rent a billboard (too costly) and state regulations limit advertising claims (which Gordon favors because they inhibit competition and reduce marketing expenses).

Gordon's best source of cold referrals is the phone book, but his ability to advertise there is limited. The directory covers the entire metropolitan area, whereas most of his patients live or work near the office. The problem, then, is that if Gordon has a large ad, most readers will be located far from his service area and won't respond to his message.

To resolve the dilemma, Gordon joins with nine other optometrists and produces a joint ad. Since each is located in a different metropolitan neighborhood, they can advertise together because their practice areas do not overlap.

PARTICIPATE IN HEALTH SCREENINGS

One of the most useful and least expensive medical evaluations is the simple health screening, a quick check of such basic concerns as weight, blood pressure and visual acuity. Dr. Gordon should participate in health screenings and such screenings should be directed toward the media.

Dr. Gordon speaks to several neighborhood health-care professionals and soon builds a screening team that includes a podiatrist, physician and hearing specialist. The health screening plan they devise features a weight check, blood pressure examination, hearing test, foot exam and visual acuity test. The program is free and available to any organization with 100 to 200 members.

At first the screenings are done locally. Sponsoring groups include civic clubs, social and fraternal organizations, professional groups, religious congregations and a college sports team. Over a period of several months the screening team holds two to three programs a month and achieves two consistent results. First, individuals with health problems are uncovered at every screening. These problems include skipped heartbeats, hearing loss, high blood pressure and inadequate visual correction. Second, although the sponsoring professionals make a point of not marketing their services overtly, the screenings provide a forum to demonstrate skills and meet new patients.

After a number of screenings, Gordon calls a local press club and offers to screen members. The club, seeing that other professional organizations have used the same program, accepts. Through contacts met at the press club, screenings are also held at newspaper offices and radio studios around the city because, after all, a screening is a good story, particularly if hidden problems are discovered. ("I had felt weak during the past several months, almost on the verge of passing out," wrote one reporter. "But other than several bouts of dizziness, nothing seemed wrong until a routine health screening turned up a surprising problem: I'm a beat skipper. My heartbeat is irregular and when a few beats are missed, too little oxygen gets to the brain.")

The screenings became annual events for most groups, and Dr. Gordon, as a result, enjoyed a continuing stream of patients and ongoing media coverage.

FIND AN ISSUE

There are many eye-care sources in the metropolitan area, including many faster and less expensive competitors than Dr. Gordon. To maintain a competitive edge, Dr. Gordon must find an issue or subject in which he can become a recognized authority.

As an amateur athlete, Dr. Gordon has long been interested in sports optometry, providing glasses, lenses and protective eyewear in such sports as basketball, handball and football.

Sports optometry is attractive, Dr. Gordon decides, because it's a subject that should interest high-school students, college athletes, and their parents, among other publics. As a first step he calls coaches at nearby high schools, junior highs and colleges with an offer to present a one-hour program on sports and eye safety.

The need for protective eyewear is apparent in basketball (because of elbows and hands near the face) and handball (the ball is so small it can squeeze between the bones above and below the eye). The need for safer vision in other sports is also obvious.

In his talks Gordon is careful to present straightforward information. He doesn't sell services, invite people to the office or list his hours. He doesn't have to. As an authority figure, people naturally gravitate toward him.

After giving lectures to various schools over a period of several months, Gordon writes to several sports editors suggesting a story on eye safety in sports. Editors are interested because Gordon has spoken on the subject and he's an eye-care professional. He also holds a controversial view: Gordon believes that all basketball and handball players at the college level and below should be required to wear protective eyewear. Gordon is a natural story and several articles result.

The articles reinforce Gordon's position as an authority figure and he finds that a regular lecture circuit evolves: Each year he speaks at least once to different school groups and each time he lectures, students and their families make appointments.

EVALUATION

Dr. Gordon should review his programming on a regular basis to see if his needs and goals are being met.

When Gordon appraises his program he sees that, for little money, he has opened new contacts, gained additional patients and produced ongoing media coverage. Perhaps most importantly, he has retained the professional image so vital to his position.

30
PROGRAM III:
Vanguard City Mortgage Bankers

Mortgage banking is a nationwide service business with competitors ranging in size from local one-man offices to corporate giants. Mortgage bankers take money from major investors such as insurance companies, and then use it to make loans for local home buyers. In addition to finding funds to finance and refinance real estate, mortgage bankers also "service" loans by collecting monthly payments, remitting funds to investors and foreclosing if required.

The Vanguard City Independent Mortgage Bankers Association is an organization with 50 local members, an executive director and a part-time secretary. Although mortgage bankers can include savings and loan associations and the mortgage departments of large real estate companies, in this association only independent firms are members. Thus the lines are drawn: independent mortgage lenders versus the S&Ls and big realty companies.

WHAT ARE THE PROBLEMS?

Five major problems are outlined in discussions with Association officers and directors.

First, national competitors have entered the local marketplace and siphoned off business. These companies have received extensive publicity because they're new, large and have full-time information staffs to attract local coverage.

Second, a computerized "do-it-yourself" mortgage center opened by a local S&L has gotten continuing print and broadcast coverage. Prospective borrowers go downtown, sit at a computer terminal and answer questions posed by a sophisticated computer program. The computer system has attracted borrowers who might otherwise use the services of Association members.

Third, a survey conducted by a local college professor, Dr. Numbers, shows 58.6 percent of all prospective home buyers think first of savings and loan associations when looking for a mortgage. Since obtaining a mortgage is a big-ticket, one-time event, being second means not getting business.

Fourth, the Numbers survey also shows 92 percent of all home buyers regard real estate brokers as the major source of financing information. This is a problem because three of the largest real estate companies in town have started their own mortgage origination departments.

Fifth, Association members are concerned that a media marketing program structured by the organization may favor one member over another. Instead, everyone wants a program that emphasizes (or creates) a difference between Association members and outside competitors.

If the public knew more about Association members and their work, the problems seen above would be less severe. A program is needed which ties mortgage bankers to home ownership in the public's eyes, a program entitled, "Mortgage Banking and You: Partners in Homeownership."

FIND THE MEDIA

The executive director shall survey all relevant media in the area to develop a contact list showing names, media affiliations, addresses and phone numbers. Estimated labor requirement: eight hours of secretarial time.

The survey shows Vanguard City is home to one major daily paper, four large suburban dailies, 28 weekly papers, 18 radio stations, one city magazine, one business weekly, six television stations, four local cable systems, and one college weekly. The daily papers and three weeklies have business sections. Two papers publish large real estate sections. Three TV stations have news operations and four produce local interview programs. The city magazine has a personal finance and real estate feature each month. The business weekly has a commercial real estate section. Two radio stations offer "all-talk" programming. Each cable outlet has local interview programming, and two cable systems make facilities available for local individuals and groups to produce their own programming. The contact list has 120 names when completed.

CREATE A MORTGAGE SURVEY

To generate ongoing media coverage, the Association should publish a weekly "Home Lender's Update" listing the names and phone numbers of each member along with rates for 30-year, 15-year, and adjustable rate mortgages (ARMs). Since the deadline for both real estate sections is Wednesday noon, updated information from members shall be required by 3 P.M. each Tuesday. Late members will be assessed $50. Members late three times in a row will be dropped from the survey for two months. Estimated labor requirement: eight hours to establish the program; two hours to update the weekly list; two hours to have it distributed to media outlets. Estimated cost: less than $45 per week for labor, paper, envelopes and postage.

The survey contains hard news and becomes a regular resource for area reporters. One real estate section runs the survey verbatim each week and several papers list the lowest rates for each loan category. Since the survey does not show information from savings and loan associations or real estate companies with mortgage departments, Association members gain an advantage over outside competitors.

WRITE A BASIC BROCHURE

Public perception is the major problem faced by the Association. The general public is largely unaware of mortgage bankers and their role in the financing process. To increase public awareness, the Association should publish a basic brochure, a competitively neutral document not favoring one member over another that describes the mortgage banking system and the general services offered by members. Estimated labor requirement: eight hours to work with a professional writer, develop copy and track production. Estimated cost: none (see below).

The Association seeks bids on the brochure from ad agencies, graphic artists and writers. In this particular situation, it selects a writer familiar with the business, rather than the lowest bidder, to develop wording. A graphic designer is chosen to lay out the brochure and work with a printer. Seventy-five thousand copies are requested by Association members. Adding 10,000 copies for its own use, the Association computes the cost of writing, designing and printing 85,000 copies, divides by 75,000 (not 85,000) and charges members according to the number of copies ordered. Using this strategy, the Association acquires 10,000 professionally written and designed brochures without cost to itself while providing a standardized document for its members.

DEVELOP A MEMBERSHIP DIRECTORY

The Association has always maintained a typewritten list of members, but a more formal document is required. A printed list should be distributed to area reporters and to the public during promotional events. Estimated cost: $50. Estimated labor requirement: virtually none.

The Association has its membership list on a computer disk, and so to make a formal copy it merely gives the disk to a member with a laser printer. There is no cost for typesetting and the printing bill totals $50. Copies for the media are enclosed with the next weekly mortgage-rate summary, thus eliminating additional postage expenses.

CREATE AN EXPERTS' ROSTER

Although a general membership list is valuable, it does not pinpoint members with specialized experience or knowledge, nor does a membership list suggest possible story ideas to reporters. The Association should create an "Experts' Roster" for distribution to the media to resolve these problems. Estimated time requirement: ten hours to identify subjects, poll members and write the listings. Estimated cost: The final list can be placed on a computer, printed on a laser device and duplicated with a copy machine for a total expense of less than $20. Copies can be sent to all media contacts.

The education committee polls the membership and finds interest in 22 subjects including such topics as "How to Get Your First Mortgage," "How to Buy at Foreclosure," "How to Speed Your Mortgage Application" and "What Really Happens at Settlement." Two lists are then established: A subject list shows topics alphabetically and members who are experts in each category. A member list shows names alphabetically and each individual's areas of expertise.

DEVELOP QUARTERLY STORY CONCEPTS

To induce additional media coverage, a committee should be formed to devise ten story ideas every three months. The concepts might be localized versions of national stories or ideas unique to Vanguard City. The story lists can then be distributed to area reporters along with the experts' roster. Estimated time requirement: about three to four hours each quarter for the committee. Estimated cost: about $25 a quarter for printing and postage.

A committee is established to produce the quarterly listings. To give some flair to the project, the quarterly lists are printed on yellow paper and becomes known as the "Yellow Sheets." Among the topics on the first listing are "New Employment Opportunities in Vanguard City Mortgage Industry," "How Washington Mortgage Rules Affect Vanguard City" and "Vanguard City Mortgage Rates Lower than Other State Areas." The lists are useful to the media and, coupled with the experts' roster, often produce stories quoting Association members.

ESTABLISH A LOCAL SPEAKERS BUREAU

Vanguard City and its surrounding suburbs are home to hundreds of civic, social and business groups. The Association should establish a speakers bureau and then contact as many organizations as possible. Estimated labor requirement: three days to compile a mailing list of target organizations, one day to send out mailers, several hours a week to respond to groups and schedule speakers. Estimated cost: about $250 for printing and postage.

The Association uses the experts' roster to find speakers and topics. Three hundred target organizations are identified from telephone listings and member contacts, and a promotional letter is then sent to each. In addition, a news release announcing the formation of the speakers bureau is sent to all media contacts.

When a speaking engagement is confirmed, the Association names both a speaker and a backup. It's understood that whoever speaks represents the Association rather than a particular company under this program. Although no promotional materials from individual firms can be distributed, copies of the basic Association brochure and membership list are provided whenever a member speaks.

ESTABLISH A MORTGAGE INFORMATION HOT LINE

There is an ongoing demand for home financing information, and to meet that demand the Association should establish a "Mortgage Information Hot Line." Such a service will allow the public to call the Association and ask general financing questions in private. Estimated labor requirement: several hours to organize the service and write a news release; several hours a week donated by members to run the service. Estimated cost: the expense of a news release plus coffee for volunteers.

To establish the Hot Line, the Association merely opens its offices from 7 P.M. to 9 P.M. on Tuesday and Thursday. Hot Line duty is rotated among officers and members. News releases are sent to the media, and fliers developed by the Association are given out from member offices. Once the project is established and calls begin coming in on a regular basis, reporters are invited to monitor the service. Several good stories promoting the Hot Line, and members of the Association, result.

Free copies of the membership list and weekly mortgage survey are offered to callers and a follow-up survey shows that a large percentage of Hot Line users ultimately contact member firms for financing. Just as importantly, the survey confirms that many callers would not have contacted member firms without the list provided through the Hot Line service.

CREATE A RADIO CALL-IN PROGRAM

Although the telephone Hot Line is a valuable public service, and while it does produce public contact and media coverage for the Association, it's necessarily limited to individual conversations that benefit a small number of people. The same conversations could be held on radio to attract a wider audience. Estimated labor requirement: three days to contact radio stations, write letters and make arrangements.

Program directors at all 18 local radio stations are contacted to suggest the call-in program. One all-talk station accepts and the show is set for a 2 P.M.–3 P.M. slot every Friday. A news release regarding the new program is sent to the media and each member distributes fliers to consumers.

The program is set up so that the Association president serves as moderator and one or two members answer questions each week. Only members who work on the telephone Hot Line are eligible to "guest" on the radio program, a policy that produces a large number of Hot Line volunteers. The basic brochure, membership list and weekly rate sheet are mentioned and sent to anyone calling the station. As an added feature, local journalists are invited on the program to discuss current issues and answer questions from the public.

HELP THOSE WITH SPECIAL NEEDS

Although the telephone Hot Line and radio program have the capacity to reach a wide audience, the hearing-impaired are excluded. To broaden its marketplace, the Association should install a TDD (Telecommunications Device for the Deaf) phone line in its offices. The TDD line can be manned during office hours and when the Hot Line is open. In addition, it could be available to any member wanting to contact individuals with TDD service. Estimated labor requirement: at least eight hours for TDD training; at least one day to develop a list of organizations that serve hearing-impaired residents. Estimated cost: about $1,000 for a TDD with a printout device and computer, or $20 for each Association member.

The Association contacts civic organizations serving the hearing-impaired for advice on establishing a TDD service. With much encouragement and support from these organizations, the service is established and a release sent to the general media as well as groups serving the hearing-impaired. The organizations not only help establish the line, but tell members about the new service as well.

In addition, the Association surveys member locations to see which ones are accessible to wheelchair users. The list is distributed to media contacts plus a variety of community groups.

What the Association discovers is that its programs not only benefit people with special needs, but that such individuals have friends and relatives who also use mortgage banking services. The program generates substantial interest in the Association from community segments underserved in the past.

ORGANIZE MEDIA BREAKFASTS

The Association and its members usually meet reporters on a business basis, often one that's formal and harried. The Association should organize a weekly media breakfast where issues can be discussed in a calm environment and where reporters and mortgage bankers can get to know one another better. Estimated labor requirement: about one hour a week to line up participants. Estimated cost: varies; in some cases reporters will pay for their own breakfasts, in others the Association will pay.

The Association decides to have a weekly media breakfast. Two or three reporters from different media outlets are invited each week along with the Association's executive director, an officer and several members. The breakfasts are held in a downtown hotel between 8 and 9:30 A.M. with 30 minutes given over to eating and the remaining time to current events. The breakfasts become popular with the media because they often produce story ideas and don't interfere with deadlines.

CREATE ALLIED-BUSINESSES PROGRAMS

Mortgage bankers depend on real estate agents and brokers for referrals and so courting the real estate community is important. The Association should establish a formal series of contacts with the real estate community to enhance its referral base. Estimated labor requirement: Ongoing. Estimated cost: minimal.

The Association checks with local real estate groups and discovers that to maintain their licenses, real estate brokers and agents must take 15 clock hours of approved continuing-education classes each year. The Association asks local realty groups to suggest topics that might interest members, forms a committee to develop course outlines, and then gets the courses approved by the state. The seminars, jointly sponsored with local realty organizations, are always packed because attendance can lead to the fulfillment of licensure requirements. The basic brochure, weekly rate summary and membership list are distributed whenever Association members lecture. Speakers are drawn from the Association's education committee and individuals listed on the experts' roster.

MEMBERSHIP DEVELOPMENT

The goal of most organizations is to expand membership. More members means more dollars to support the group's goals and more people to carry out its functions. However, since the members of the Association compete not only with nonmembers but also among themselves for a limited volume of business, and since the Association already has enough members to carry out its functions, no effort should be made to dilute benefits by expanding the membership. Conversely, membership should not be denied to any interested party that meets the standards established for all current members. Estimated labor requirement: none. Estimated cost: none.

The Association makes no effort to solicit additional members and few firms apply.

CREATE A CONSUMER LIBRARY

Although local libraries have extensive personal finance and real estate collections, the Association should establish a specialized mortgage lending library. Books, magazines and industry reports can be solicited from members. Estimated labor requirement: uncertain. Some time will be required to coordinate material donations and write a news release. Additional time will be needed to oversee collection when in use.

The library is established at the Association's offices. A news release sent to the media notes that it's available on an appointment-only basis to journalists and the public. Although not used frequently, the library does receive notice in several area publications.

CREATE A PREMIUM

Premiums are often offered to prospective clients in many fields as an inducement to obtain their time, attention and business. To attract attention, the Association should either buy or produce a handbook that offers value to potential borrowers but represents a small cost to Association members.

The Association contacts several publishers and finds one who offers "How to Save Money When Financing Your Home" in bulk. If the publisher puts the Association's name, address, phone number and current membership roster in the publication, the Association will buy a special printing of 5,000 copies at discount.

Once the copies are purchased, a release announcing their availability through member firms and without charge is sent to all media contacts. Over a period of several weeks, nearly all the copies are distributed to consumers, which means almost 5,000 people have direct contact with member firms.

USE AN OUTSIDE SPEAKER

The Association can benefit from a program which introduces the independent mortgage banking community directly to the public. Such a program must be consumer oriented, informational and of sufficient interest to attract media coverage, thereby multiplying the program's value. An educational seminar, presented by someone outside the local mortgage banking industry but with extensive consumer credentials, could meet these requirements.

Title: The program must be current without being

overly specific. "Home Finance Today: How to Cut the Cost of Real Estate Mortgages in Half" might be a good title.

The speaker should explain how the mortgage market works, how strong loan applications can be developed and how borrowers can save tens of thousands of dollars, if not more, through such strategies as careful mortgage selection, the use of prepayments, curtailments, refinancing, external saving accounts and short-term financing.

To give a local flavor to the program, an Association officer should present a brief overview of current interest rates in Vanguard City and recent mortgage trends.

Location: The program must be held in a setting with sufficient transportation, parking and public facilities to assure participant comfort and safety, including access for the handicapped. A hotel or motel are typical choices, but an attractive high-school auditorium or a religious facility could be equally acceptable and perhaps less expensive.

Sponsors: Association members will be identified as "sponsors" and each will receive a specified number of seminar tickets as well as recognition in the seminar program guide.

Tickets: Admission will be by ticket only. There are three basic ways to distribute tickets:

First, Association members can log consumer contacts several weeks prior to the seminar and then call each contact ten days before the program to see who wants to attend. This process not only gives members a nonselling reason to call possible borrowers, but also identifies prospects no longer looking for loans.

Second, tickets can be given to regular clients, those frequently in the market for financing.

Third, tickets can be given to real estate brokers and agents, traditionally the industry's largest referral source. The brokers and agents, in turn, can pass the tickets to prospective purchasers (and, hopefully, eventual borrowers).

In each case the offer of tickets to an institutional presentation creates opportunities to demonstrate goodwill and enhance credibility.

The number of tickets available to each sponsor will

depend on the meeting facility's size and the number of sponsors participating in the program.

Timing: The program is best given on a weekday evening from 7:30 to 9:30 and divided into two sections with a brief break at midpoint, as follows:

7:00–7:29: REGISTRATION

7:30–7:39: INTRODUCTION BY ASSOCIATION OFFICER

7:40–8:30: SPEAKER

8:30–8:40: BREAK

8:41–9:00: SPEAKER

9:01–9:10: ASSOCIATION OFFICER PRESENTS LOCAL TRENDS

9:11–9:29: QUESTIONS AND ANSWERS

9:30: CLOSE BY ASSOCIATION OFFICER

Note that although the program is scheduled to end at 9:30, the question-and-answer period may continue until 9:45 or 10: or possibly later, a factor which should be considered when renting space.

Promotion: Efforts to promote the program should begin four to six weeks before the event. Promotion should include the distribution of a cover letter, news release, program outline and speaker biography to media contacts, civic groups and local real estate organizations.

Advertising: The association should establish an advertising campaign noting when tickets will be available from member sponsors, possibly one or two ads in local realty sections. The promotional purpose of such ads is to place the Association before the public and help assure the broad distribution of tickets.

Handouts: Only institutional handouts, such as the basic Association brochure, membership roster and weekly rate report should be distributed at the seminar. Materials from individual firms and on-site solicitations will be forbidden.

Speaker Criteria: The oratorical skills of a William Jennings Bryan are not necessary for a seminar program, though such qualities are surely desirable. Instead, the Association needs a speaker with three specific attributes.

First, the speaker must be a credible individual, someone recognized as an authority figure in the field. Such an individual could be a local mortgage banker, at least in theory, but in practice a local person is unlikely to work because (A) he (or she) is local and therefore not especially unique to the media, and (B) a local person competes with other Association members. What is needed, then, is someone from out of town.

Second, the Association needs someone with good communication skills, an individual who represents a good story to the media.

Third, promoting this event will be far easier if the speaker is well known and media-wise.

Public Participation: A sense of participation can be created by allowing audience members to ask questions. A card for written questions can be placed on each seat and then passed up at intermission or to staffers working the aisles during the program. The questions, in turn, can be read from the podium by an Association officer. This process creates the aura of participation, gives variety to the program and, not incidentally, allows the Association to avoid loud or ego-centered questioners.

Staffing: The Association should handle all ticket requests, have personnel available for registration at the seminar, pickup questions from the audience and do such promotional calling and mailing as may be required. In addition, Association officers will introduce the guest, speak on local rates, summarize loan preferences and trends, read questions from the audience and close the program.

Budgeting: In evaluating a budget it must be recognized that the total cost will be divided by the membership and that the Association itself will incur only minor, out-of-pocket costs. If, for example, there are 50 member/sponsors, the cost to participate will be only $226 per sponsor within the projected budget below, hardly an extravagant expense when one considers what the average mortgage banker spends yearly for advertising and media relations.

Alternatively, sponsorship fees can be set above actual costs to compensate the Association for organizing and promoting the program. A sponsorship fee of $250 or $300 is reasonable.

A projected budget might include the following costs:

Speaking fee	$5,000
Hotel and transportation	600
Site rental	750
Advertising	2,000
Printing	200
Reception	2,500
Staff overtime	100
Stamps, telephone, etc.	150
TOTAL	$11,300

As an alternative to a flat fee, the Association may instead wish to charge members for tickets. If 1,250 seats are available, then each ticket can be priced at $9.05 and offered to members on a first come, first serve basis.

A committee is established to oversee the program and pick a speaker. It takes several months and many meetings to organize the program, but here's what happened.

After reviewing several choices, the seminar committee decided to invite a well-known real estate professor who just published a book on home financing.

Since the public was not being charged admission, the Association found it could rent a suburban high-school auditorium that was centrally located and offered extensive parking plus access for the handicapped.

Several news releases were sent to media contacts, three ads ran in the major daily, and prior to the program, a small reception was held in a local hotel for the speaker, media contacts and Association officers and directors.

With strong demand, it was decided each member would pay a flat fee and receive a set number of tickets. Most members used the tickets as premiums for prospective clients, real estate brokers and investors.

The Association required the speaker to arrive a day early for media interviews it arranged. A car and escort were provided to drive the speaker to unfamiliar locations.

The speech was well-covered by the media with several

pre-event stories, plus articles on the speech itself. In addition, a radio interview arranged by the Association received many calls.

The Association achieved three major goals. Its name was used repeatedly in connection with the program. The concept of mortgage banking was explained in many articles and broadcasts. And, perhaps most importantly, the membership had a non-adversarial reason to contact prospects and potential business sources.

Following its experience with the first speaker, the Association established a semiannual speaker program with one speech held in mid-March and another scheduled for September. Having programs on a regular basis created two major news events each year that produced extensive atten-·tion for the Association and its members—attention which came just at the start of the major "seasons" when business was most active.

EVALUATION AND MONITORING

The media marketing program established by the Association is a long-term, ongoing effort which should be administered and reviewed by a standing committee. The program should be adjusted and refined over time as the Association becomes more experienced with media marketing programs and as member interests evolve.

The Association creates a media marketing committee to oversee its projects, polls members every six months to get their reactions to the program, solicits ideas for new projects and files news articles about the Association and its members in the library. The local professor, Dr. Numbers, is hired to produce an annual consumer attitude survey.

Over time the Association's members increase their share of the market. They become better known to the public and the concept of mortgage banking becomes less murky. Reporters call more frequently than in the past and subsequently there are more stories about Association members. The outreach seminars to real estate groups prove successful and the general demand for speakers grows. The radio program and weekly rate sheets give the group ongoing media coverage, while the semiannual speaker's program and occasional premiums attract interest at times that might otherwise be slack.

- 30 -

INDEX